FROM BUTLINS TO BEIJING

Brian Banham

Copyright Brian Banham © 2014

Published by

All rights reserved. No part of this book may be reproduced, adapted, stored in a retrieval system or transmitted by any means, electronic, mechanical, photocopying, or otherwise without the prior written permission of the author.

The rights of Brian Banham to be identified as the author of this work have been asserted in accordance with the Copyright, Designs and Patents Act 1988.

ISBN: 978-1515031789

Layout by Ebooks by Design

FOREWORD

My family and several friends have often said I should write about my life. I think this is because I have had a varied life with much wandering in the early days before I came into contact with Mary, my lovely wife. She has set me on an even keel even though it took some time, many different jobs and travel, in our early relationship.

So I still consider that the most exciting and dangerous time was in 1959 when I, with four other people set out to go to the Mediterranean for the winter on a yacht converted from a fishing boat, perhaps the only reason I am still here because it had an eight foot draught and we encountered some ferocious weather. I open my book with this and follow on from memories from three years of age and living in Norfolk.

CHAPTER 1

Time clutters the memory, and experiences, which were of extraordinary importance when they occurred, tend to lose that importance.

The way of life for everyone has changed dramatically during the last fifty odd years and conditions, personal requirements, acceptance of professions, particularly those that concern people's well-being, both physical and psychologically, are regarded as much more commonplace than they were when my occupation was an unusual one, as resident palmist for Butlin's Holiday Camp at Skegness.

I had spent some seasons at Skeggy, living in a caravan across from the camp and I had decided to give the profession a rest for the winter of 1959 and visit Spain, which I was convinced was permanently sunny. I planned to go with the press photographer, a splendid square-jawed hunk named Tony Brand.

We started to make our plans for a touring holiday to begin about the end of September when we would travel light on his motor bike. Neither of us gave a thought to language, passports, pesetas or where we would go. Early in August a very attractive girl had arrived on my caravan site in an open topped convertible Jaguar car, and settled into a van just across from mine.

I was writing up my 'palms' at the time and waved to her from my window. I should explain, my palm reading took a very practical form. I would take an impression of my client's right hand, (left for inheritance) painting it with a rather sticky oil-based white paint, take their names and date of birth on one of my prepared black sheets of paper stating my name "Professor Bada" and which also had listed characteristics, which I would tick in my readings. 'He that knows himself knows most'. Then whilst wiping off the paint with cotton wool would spend a few moments talking to them during which time any reaction I had would help me with my observations. There were two options which a client could have, a character study or that plus a prediction for the coming year.

The pretty girl responded with a broad smile and wave and then walked off towards the camp. Later that evening I saw her behind the counter in the service canteen. I would often use the canteen to write up my forecast for clients whilst enjoying a coffee and Lincolnshire bun.

She was immediately popular at the camp and I would watch a steady stream of young men arrange their plumage and preen their wings, but, Beth, that was her name, fell for a young Irish Redcoat named Dave Allen who sported a short first finger and did a variety of crazy knockabout and tumble acts – obviously destined for stardom. The young handsome comedian, however was romantically involved with one of the Rowe sisters, Table Tennis twins who worked there and were at that time, Pairs Champions of Great Britain, and very seldom did his eyes look upon Beth with anything other than gratefulness for a cup of tea or a Lincolnshire Bun, as she bravely held back the tears and said, "next please".

My working hours were long, every day and evening except Saturday when it was change-over day. I had my desk at the rear of the main ballroom. I got a lot of publicity from Joe Daniels and his Hotshots, who were the resident band. My real publicity though was on Saturday evening when the "Who's Who" would be held in the main theatre. All the new campers would go to the show and there were two sittings to accommodate them. All the personalities that worked at the camp would be introduced. Dave Allen was the compare on several occasions and he and I worked out a patter for when I was introduced.

I had grown a beard, reddish, usually wore the most colourful clothes I could find in Skegness and also had a long black cloak. I would stand on stage on one side of it, resplendent in my cloak and stare at the audience. Dave would give his introduction – "Professor Bada knows more about you than you know yourself". He would invite, usually a young woman from the audience to come up, chat her up a bit and she would then give me her hand, I would look at it and tell the month of her birth. Dave and I had perfected a simple code which gave me a lead. In his questioning of the girl he would find out her month and then he announced that I would now look at the hand. I would usually hesitate and offer two months, then after a bit of deliberation would give her correct month. This had a great effect and after the show I would go back to my desk where there would be a queue waiting to have their palms read. In some instances I was able to give some clear advice, useful forecasts, apt observations. Some people had complete faith in my readings, one woman asked me, if I read her daughter's hand could I tell her who had stolen her duffle coat.

Palmistry (Chiromancy) of any worth must come from an honest attempt to understand the mystery of the hand. I didn't want to impress, astonish, or control another human being. My predictions of future events, whilst difficult, were in the main general. I saw it as a 'Folk-Psychology', and did my best to help my clients.

It was a very interesting time at Butlins. We all worked very hard to make everyone's holiday exciting. As the season was short it was necessary to earn as much as possible in the four months of the season. I had a portable desk which I would take down to the beach on hot days, I also set it up beside the large swimming pool, and I judged various competitions, sometimes with Dave, sometimes the Head of Entertainment, The Cricket Coach, Soccer Coach, and other personalities. It was a great way to get publicity. We had a host of competitions; Knobbly Knees, Glamorous Grannies, Beauty Queen of the week, Miss England heats, etc. Butlins was a flourishing business and I had a concession, which meant I paid Butlins a third of my income.

Our own, the staff relaxation, was usually at a farm near the camp after everything closed down on Friday nights. One of the hairdressers on the camp was the daughter of the farmer and the family enjoyed the parties there. They were pretty wild, having watched the campers enjoy themselves for a week we tried to catch up in one night. Their pigs fed on a sort of ecstasy did strange things!

My caravan was a four berth job and sometimes Beth would arrive back late see my light on and come and visit and occasionally would stay at the other end of the van. As her love for Dave grew stronger and it was unrequited, she became sadder and knowing our plans for the winter, one day said she would like to come with us, throwing in for good measure her Jaguar as a means of transport.

We discussed this suggestion late one night over some gin and tonics and arrived at the practical conclusion that it would 'indeed be very sensible'. No mention was made of the Jules et Jim content, neither Tony nor I were contemplating a romantic association with Beth at that time as there were several hundred holidaymakers each week, a high proportion of them being unattached girls and everyone who rated as staff, particularly those in the public eye, were in great demand.

For Beth, Butlins was the first time she had been allowed to leave the family fold and go her own way, other than boarding school, and at the age of 18 she had obviously put up a good proposition to get her parents to agree for her to work there. I suppose being an only child had something to do with it, anyway she wrote to her parents and told them she was planning to go to Spain for the winter with two young men, she gave us both a glowing report as to our respectability and assured them that we would take good care of her.

Tony and I had accepted the fact that Beth was coming, he made plans to sell his motor bike so we were somewhat surprised to be told by Beth a few days later that her father, a Steel Magnate in the Midlands, did not like the idea of her going and had, on receipt of her letter conceived an idea for a winter's cruise in the Med. He bought a yacht converted from a fishing smack and invited Tony and me to his home, Broseley Hall, in Iron Bridge to interview us as potential crew.

We spent 2/6d on *The Observer Book of Sailing* and learnt terms like 'jib, mainsail and rudder'. We needn't have bothered as he didn't understand much about sailing either, although he had bought charts of every inch of the Med. He was an incredible man; apparently on receipt of Beth's letter telling him of our plans he decided to tour the Med to arrange ports of call for a holiday venture. He intended to build a fleet of three steel hulled pleasure boats and create holiday cruises for three months for wealthy people that wanted to avoid the English winter. After some discussion on our suitability, he decided that we were to be potential sailors and agreed to us becoming crew on the journey.

We had a marvellous overnight stay in Broseley Hall, a lovely old house set in picturesque countryside on the outskirts of the small town, Iron Bridge. Mrs Dixon had an old Rolls Royce, which she used for shopping, Mr (Bill) Dixon had a red Jaguar and Beth's open Jaguar filled the front parking spaces. Tony's motorbike looked a little out of place in all the affluence. Having been royally treated to some excellent hospitality we climbed on his motorbike and raced back through the Midlands countryside singing sea shanties. Beth stayed at home to prepare for our arrival two weeks later. She had taken my guitar and some of our clothes in her car in readiness for our trip.

Looking back now I cannot remember what we had arranged in terms of passports, medical care and all those things which today are very much part of my travel around the world in the oil industry.

I suppose Beth's father arranged all the necessary support. The last two weeks dragged past. I sent all my spare cash to my Aunt in Norwich, I didn't have a bank account at that time, bought some premium bonds and sent my few belongings to her for safe keeping until my return.

I returned my caravan to Barbara and Allen from whom I had leased it, and said goodbye to the many friends at Butlins. During that two week period Tony would often be found in the bar relating his sailing expertise to anyone that would listen – he had rowed across Chichester Harbour. He had convinced himself that this trip would be an extension of his previous experience.

Well good bye to what was a fairly primitive life, although not without its romantic appeal. My Gipsy friend who came round to the caravan park every Friday morning and read my thumb, which I would push out of the door as I lay in bed, said that I needed care. I was going into an unknown situation. I guess I somehow knew that, but it did give me a few moments thought on what a very challenging period it would be.

On my last day I looked fondly around Butlins and wondered if this would be my last time here, Tony was in the same frame of mind. The season was drawing to a close and the prospect of a winter spent cruising in the warmth of the Med was very appealing. We set off with very few belongings, what we did have were either strapped to me or the motor bike. He had decided to keep it for a while as we now knew that we would possibly spend up to four weeks in Aberystwyth where the boat was moored, as it had to be painted with a special coating to withstand the bugs in the Med, this could only be done when the tide was out. As our yacht had an eight foot draught, it also needed good high tides and they were more suitable at the end of September or early October.

I thrust my hands deep into my trench coat pockets leaned on Tony and watched the hedgerows sweep past as we raced towards Broseley, we cleared Lincolnshire, Derbyshire, and various English counties until we reached Iron Bridge, where Mr Dixon had his factory. I had often wondered about Iron Bridge, how did it come to get this name, what was its origin? The town was dominated by an iron bridge, in those days dirty and uncared for, crossing the river, and the town has grown up around it.

We arrived at the Hall, a Queen Anne House, square with typical greystone exterior that is so popular in that part of the country, to be met by the family. We were now on a different footing with them, we were to be very closely knit for several months. Mrs Dixon was charming, a warm sympathetic lady, gentle and artistic, She showed us around the house, it was very impressive. We were shown our bedroom, twin beds, did we mind sharing? Not at all.

During dinner that night we got down to serious discussions of the proposed Mediterranean cruise. Bill Dixon outlined his plans in far more detail than when we had previously met him. He was going to build a small fleet of three steel hulled yachts, each would have a captain and crew and would be designed with the best accommodation possible, a top class chef, leisure facilities including a small pool, and a games room. The boats would travel in convoy with the very latest means of communicating with each other. The holiday cruise would be of three months duration, very expensive and would be located in the Med.

He wanted to spend the winter there checking all the navigational details, ensuring of supplies of provisions and generally creating a route, which would offer a holiday of leisure, sightseeing and gastronomic delights.

I wanted to be on that cruise, I was inwardly very excited. It was the most attractive proposition I had ever been given. Later that night as we were preparing for bed Tony said he felt the same, Spain, France, Italy etc., all places we had only read about. I slept, but was in a constant state of excitement.

We spent the next day packing their van and on the Saturday we all set off for Aberystwyth in convoy, Mr and Mrs Dixon in his Jaguar, Beth driving the van, with Tony and me keeping her company in the front. Tony's motorbike was strapped into the van – we knew we would need it in Aberystwyth.

We followed a very winding road through Shropshire and entered Wales. We were making good time when a dog ran across a very narrow road in front of us, and Beth, swerved, then followed it and placed the van in a ditch. The three of us clambered out of the cab which had a 45% list to port or starboard – I had not yet become a real sailor, so how was I to know? Bill Dixon returned to find us and we deliberated as to what should be done. Our problems were solved when an enormously fat Welshman with wisps of corn in his hair from his laden trailer, arrived and decided he would rescue us and pull the van out with his tractor.

This took some time and eventually it was righted, but, with a bent driver's side door and the passenger seating somewhat awry. Tony and I were offered seats in the Jaguar and once more we set off.

After some miles of steady driving, Mr Dixon was overtaking an even slower car when he had to pull in rather quickly and the bumper of his Jag somehow caught the bumper of the other car and pulled it off. Angry words were exchanged while Tony and I tried to be serious. In the midst of insurance exchanges I was suddenly horrified to think that I had only been with this family a few hours and we had experienced two crashes. I said to Tony, "Tragedies always come in threes, me being a fortune teller and all that"!! He took me seriously and was very uncomfortable for the rest of the journey, which luckily was uneventful.

We parked the battered van and Jag on the quayside and I took my first look at what was to be my immediate home and possibly my home for six months. She was a 45 foot Bermudan rigged, sharp at both ends, ex fishing smack, powered by two petrol/paraffin Kelvin engines. She looked in good condition and there was a nice flat area on top for sun bathing, we noted.

The main cabin with rudder and all the bits had ample space for two people and directly below was a 'sitting room' with dining table. Tony and my bedroom was up front, we had two single beds running along the inner wall to a very small ladder and porthole for easy exit.

Mr and Mrs Dixon had a bedroom between us and the cabin, Beth's room was alongside theirs. There was plenty of storage space and we started carefully loading all the provisions we had brought including the special paint for the hull of the boat.

We were beginning to form a rather excited relationship, and talking of sunshine and Spanish wine, Flamenco dancing and garlic in France. The weekend passed in rapid time, we were introduced to Bill Lucas who was the local engineer. Bill Dixon had arranged for him to work on the Yacht, overhauling and checking all the moving parts and ensuring she was seaworthy.

Bill was a splendid man and during the next weeks Tony and I became very friendly with him and learnt a great deal about handling a boat and sail, albeit on land as it were. The Dixon's came down each weekend bringing with them every conceivable item that we might need during our cruise.

As our friendship grew with Bill he would often say over a pint in our most philosophical moments that we were definitely of the "fools rush in where angels fear to tread" variety, and he was very concerned for our safety on the eventual trip.

However, on our first Monday on the Yacht after the Dixons had departed for Broseley we discussed as many aspects of the situation as we could, we worked out when the tides would be out each day to enable us to start work on the hull and we also decided to apply to the local Employment Office for any benefit which we were due.

We put on our most impressive clothes, climbed on Tony's bike and went into the small town.

We found the Employment Exchange and presented ourselves to a small round faced girl and told her we were out of work and looking for assistance. We were shown into a spare room with partitions on which was pasted the odd poster giving advice on what to do with your life and eventually a thin, wispy-haired man appeared and gave us forms to fill in.

I asked him if this was necessary as we were only staying in the town a few weeks, we weren't particularly looking for work, only dole benefits. He said the first thing to do before he could have any sensible conversation with us was to fill in as much of the form as possible.

We were left alone in the room and we fell about with some of the questions, particularly those asking for the type of work we were suitable for. I, true to my profession requested Palm Reading and signed myself as *Professor Bada*, brackets *(Professional Name)*. Tony provided *Portrait and Press Photographer, specialising in pretty children and prettier ladies.*

We sat and waited, our mirth slowly evaporating, eventually he came back and I remarked, "Business not very brisk."

He said that it was near the end of the season and it would soon be quite busy. He looked at my application form and we waited with baited breath for the job request to sink in. He didn't bat an eyelid, after he had looked at them both he said to me "Are you really a professor? Because you're not entitled to call yourself that unless you are!" Not stopping for a reply he said to Tony, "Are you a qualified Photographer?"

Tony indignantly retorted that he was and he had photographed some of the leading personalities in the film and social world, when the man said "You won't get any benefit unless you are prepared to work."

We replied in unison, "We are, we are."

I asked if he could find me a job reading palms, because if he could I would start tomorrow. He replied the only work he had listed was labouring on a new building site behind the town and unless we were prepared to work there he couldn't give us any benefit, and, he added, we both looked healthy.

We looked at each other, and we both knew there was no possibility of us humping bricks and cement around with men with handkerchiefs on their heads, tied at their corners, that had little appeal, but we agreed to visit the site. He said to call in again at the same time the next day when he would give us the necessary details and directions. Meanwhile he would contact the site foreman to expect us about 9.30am.

"9.30?" We asked amazed.

"Yes, if you call here just after nine I will have it ready".

We left the building, the weight of bureaucracy heavy on our shoulders. That night we joined the local 'mens working club' which was a laugh, and played snooker, drank several pints and didn't talk much.

After getting back to the Yacht *My Amour*, our normal good humour took over. Here we were, two young irresponsible men, living in the lap of luxury, all found, with no one to answer to, at least until the weekend. We decided that we would live it up, local girls back on the yacht each night, drink when we felt like it and to hell with the labour exchange. I got out my guitar and played my three chords to every song we could think of with some emphasis on seas shanties. Later we were inspired. Yes, we would go to the building site and apply for work, so we searched through all our clothes.

The next morning two gaily coloured 'sailors' emerged from our floating home, climbed the ladder and with some difficulty got on Tony's bike.

I had on my open-toed sandals, no socks, green knee length shorts and a vivid blue loose fitting open necked shirt with short sleeves, which I had sometimes worn when judging the weeks Beauty Queen Competition at Butlins, a red beret, which I had worn as a young man in Norfolk, and it had never left me, finished off with a raffia basket with a shoulder strap that Beth had left on the boat.

Tony looked equally resplendent in yellow canvass shoes, red white and blue rugger socks, white shorts, blue tee shirt, which showed off to perfection his hairy chest and a sombrero which he had bought in anticipation of our Spanish holiday, and he also had a shoulder bag.

We set off for the labour Exchange, as we swept out of the harbour, Bill Lucas was walking in carrying a bag of tools, he screamed with delight and threw the bag at us shouting, "Get yer knickers off you pouffs!"

At the labour exchange a look of amazement came over the young girls' face as she realised who we were. "Please don't let Mr Davies see you like that," she said, "you will ruin all our lives here."

"Like what I asked?"

But she didn't reply, rushing through to the other office and come back with some forms. She told us how to get to the site; we said we would come back and let them know he we got on.

We left her with a great grin on her face. We found our way up to the site on the bike, passing on our way several people who stopped in their tracks to stare at us. We parked the bike just past the site and started to slowly mince our way up the centre track. Houses were being built on either side of the track and there were some workmen doing various jobs on several of them. At the top of the track we could see the foreman's site office.

Whistles started to come from workmen that were in the first houses and suddenly the place was echoing to wolf whistles, catcalls and comments. "Look what we have here boyo," screamed from a first floor window has stayed with me. "Quick lads, there's sartorial perfection for you!" The Welsh have a great ability to link a situation with humour.

We smiled at the workmen and continued mincing up the track. I was swinging my shoulder basket and Tony kept flicking his hair, he overdid it a bit putting one hand on his hip as he walked. We arrived at the site office which was surrounded by building debris including some twisted pipe work and a very old Heinz Baked Beans advertisement, which transported me back in years to a short period of my life when I had been a maintenance engineer on their night shift.

On the door were the words, Cruds keep out man asleep. Tony pushed open the door, the room stank of stale cigarettes. There were two men inside, both with fags dangling from their faces sitting on either side of a small table. They looked up and stared, gradually one's face started to crumble, first the eyes, then the mouth, then he suddenly smashed the table with his fist. "Fuck me boys, Davy, what is it?"

"No fuck them Ivor, after you with the blond one".

I smiled, lisping, "Who is the foreman pleath?"

"Yeth," said Tony, "we want a word with the both". He swept his hand over his blond locks and smiled, his great open face alight with warmth and friendship.

Tony was, as he often said, a cross between Rock Hudson and Burt Lancaster and he had a great deal of charm.

"What is this boys," said Davy "are you starting a cabaret?"

"No we've come for a job" I said

"What sort of job", he asks getting a bit tight around the mouth

"What jobs have you got?" I enquired, "We've just come from Skegness and we are looking for work".

"What have you been doing?" said Ivor, still holding back from an explosion of laughter.

"Well I've been the 'camp' photographer, at Butlins," said Tony.

I was about to say I was a Professor when Ivor let out a scream of laughter, started rocking back and forth in his chair then suddenly jumped to his feet and rushed out of the office.

"Now look what you've done," said Davy, "get the hell out of here you clever bastards"

"What do you mean?" said Tony, "we've been sent by the labour exchange to –"

"Shut up, piss off before I set the boys on you. Go back to bloody Butlins you pansies."

I smiled and said, "There are three kinds of turds I don't like in life, mustard, custard, and you, you big thit" and we hi-tailed it out of the office and sprinted down to our bike. The chorus of catcalls from the houses echoed after us, we got on the bike and belted down to the town.

When we arrived at the labour exchange and parked the bike, we had a chance to talk about the whole episode.

"Phew" said Tony still somewhat flushed, "that could have been nasty."

"You're not kidding" I said, "I guessed from the start he had us sussed out."

"Nasty piece of work" said Tony as he took off his shoulder bag and put it in the saddlebag on the bike.

"Glad he didn't ask us to stay," I said, "wouldn't fancy working for him."

We both started to giggle.

"That was funny," said Tony, now feeling safe, "the other guy was a knockout, I bet he shit himself with laughing, the stench on that site must be awful – glad I'm not working there." The tears started to roll down his face, "Hey we can't go to old Davies like this, let's go back to the boat and change."

We climbed back on the bike, I stuck both legs out like a *v* on either side of Tony and we weaved off shouting "A sailors life for me ha ha". He drove the bike down the middle of the esplanade weaving in and out of the white lines in the road, we arrived back at the boat and were just about to descend our ladder when a police car drew up next to the bike and two policemen got out. The driver asked "Is that your bike son?"

"Yes," said Tony.

"Have you got a driving licence?"

"Yes" said Tony. "Have you got your green owners card?"

"Yes."

"Can I see it?"

I was standing half-way on the ladder with my face at a level with the policeman's crutch, "Why?" I asked.

"Did I ask you," he said.

"No."

"Well shut up."

"Do you have a reason for questioning Tony" I said. "What's he done?"

"I am interested in your curly haired friend if he's the owner I want to see his licence. He's going to show it to me aren't you, sonny?"

Tony fumbled in his bag, "Forget it professor I'll deal with this." He got out his wallet and after a show of fumbling gave the driving licence to the policeman. "My green card is on the boat I will get it."

I climbed up and sat on the bollard our boat was tied too. The other policeman said to me "What have you come as?"

"What do you mean" I said.

"You know."

"I haven't a clue" I said. "Why the outfit?"

"This is no outfit, it's my summer gear."

"I'd hate to see you spring outfit," said the driver. "Do you own this boat."

"No" I said, "it belongs to a Mr Dixon, we are crew looking after it until it goes round the Med carrying the flag of Aberystwyth, The Mayor of the town is aware of this and if you need confirmation I suggest you get in touch with Bill Lucas who I am sure you know – everyone else in this town does."

I started to go down the ladder but Tony was coming up holding his form, he got to the top and I went down, I saw my camera swinging on its hook through the glass screen and I suddenly thought, this is the most wonderful photo, Tony in his gear being interviewed by the police

I went into the cabin, checked the film and the light-meter, came out, started climbing the ladder and saw the police car driving off with Tony on the back seat. I stood for some minutes looking into space, wondering what Tony could have done to warrant his arrest. I climbed back onto the boat, what would the Dixon's think, this was our second day alone and already we were in trouble with the police. *Bill Lucas, he's the man.* I shut the cabin door and raced up the ladder. I remembered we had seen Bill earlier going further down the quayside. I ran along the seven other boats and at the fourth I heard knocking, went down and shouted, "Bill!" He appeared looking a bit haggard with a large hammer in his hand. "Bill! The cops have arrested Tony."

"What for?"

"I don't know. What can I do?"

Bill smiled. "Its probably because of the way you were dressed this morning. What happened?"

I told him of our experience and he said, "That Davy has a brother in law that's a cop, I bet he set Tony up."

I said, "I'm going on the bike to the police station and see what I can do."

"I would change if I were you," said Bill, "That gear won't impress them."

I went back to the boat and changed into my fawn trousers and half sweater, went up the ladder and climbed on the bike. The key was still in it, started to drive it out of the entrance only to see Tony walking back in. "What happened?"

"When we got nearly up to the town hall, they said I had been driving without due care and attention and if I did it again they would have me, pushed me out of the car and told me to piss off."

"You're kidding" I said.

"They treated the whole thing as a joke."

"Bill thinks it's that Dave at the building site, his brother in law is a cop. All I know is we don't need to cross them anymore"

"Yeah", said Tony, "I was a bit scared though".

We climbed back down to the boat, the tide was rapidly going out, *My Amour* was leaning on the harbour wall. "Let's have something to eat then start scraping the hull".

We were about to start when Tony said "Hey what about the labour exchange?"

"Crikey, I had forgot! Let's go."

We parked outside and went in, the young girl smiled at us and said "Hold on I will get Mr Davies for you."

We sat down on the two chairs in the office, she came back and said, "Go into the next room and he will see you." We shuffled in trying to look eager for work.

Mr Davies came out and asked us to sit down. "I hear you were very rude to the foreman at the building site."

"No Mr Davies," I said, "he was rude to us and a bit threatening."

"Is that a formal complaint you're making", he asked.

"No. It was an observation, we didn't get a good welcome and he told us, not very politely to get out."

"Well he wasn't pleased with either of you and said he wouldn't employ you if you were the last people in the town."

"Well we are sorry to hear that," we said in unison, "what do we do now?"

"I will put in an application for you both, but, you must be prepared to take any work that I can offer."

"We are," we said, "what should we do?"

"Leave me your telephone number."

"We don't have one."

"What's your address?"

We told him and he suggested we come into the exchange on a regular basis to keep tabs on possible work, we thanked him and sidled out.

As we drove off, I said, "that's not very satisfactory come to think of it, we haven't actually got anything in writing, re getting any benefit."

"Well" says Tony, "he's got all our info if we get anything out of it count it as a bonus. The Dixon's have left us plenty of food all we have to buy is fresh bread and milk."

The harbour was empty, it was a very deep harbour when the tide was fully in, able to take a boat like ours with an eight foot draught. The mud where the sea had been was thick and we sloshed around in it and started scraping the hull. This was hard work and we took several little breaks. I started at the front, Tony at the rear.

"How are we going to get the side on the wall done?" Tony asked.

"Dunno, maybe Bill has some ideas."

Days went by each one having its own point of interest and each one with a natural time change to suit the tide as we scraped away at the hull of the boat to clean it in readiness for the special paint. It was dirty work and sometimes quite smelly as at times we were up to our knees in sea water when we started each day, to be replaced by a slippery green bottom of the harbour intermingled with rocks and stones as the tide went out. Usually we worked for about four hours sometimes singing, sometimes groaning.

It took all of three weeks to get the boat done. I had discovered a natural pool about ten feet long by four wide and four feet deep just outside the harbour wall in which I washed in each day after the tide had gone out. It suited me fine as I was not a great swimmer; I think the furthest I had ever swum was about two lengths of a beer glass on my back at Skegness. I didn't always dry myself after my dip as I wanted to get brown and I'd remembered a chap in the RAF from Brighton who was always brown. He said if you left seawater on your body the skin would easily turn brown. I don't think this was true with me – however I persisted, sometimes walking back to the boat shivering with cold and crusty eyed from the salt.

We were both healthy and looking tanned from either the odd sunny day or the sea spray. Once a week we both went to the town baths and cleaned off the oil stains. Our nights were great fun. We often went to the university dances, or those in the town hall; our standing with the local girls was brilliant – we could offer parties on a yacht. We both took full advantage of our situation and shared many a night with the locals, sometimes including Bill. We also played snooker at the working men's club. We got some benefit from Mr Davies after two weeks of waiting, and he didn't suggest we go for any other jobs. "Nothing suitable", he said several times when we dropped in to check.

The first Wednesday of our stay was our first dance night, and it produced what Tony called my 'Religious Experience'. Fortifying ourselves with a 'jar or two' in the working men's club we steamed up to the town hall on Tony's bike and having paid to get in were surprised by the amount of talent around. Several girls, apparently students back at the university after the summer recess were standing around, Tony quickly whisked one off, no doubt impressing her with his lunging style of modern dance and his 'sailors' chat. I took my time and wandered up to the balcony to survey the scene. I was particularly taken with a dark haired woman of perhaps thirty who was sitting by herself on the balcony just across from me. I tried to catch her eye but that ploy was interrupted when a red haired young man asked her to dance, which she accepted. I sat out the next three numbers watching a fairly full floor of dancers move round and round. Most couples had a respectable distance between their bodies, but not Tony, he was well wrapped up with his girl and his big beaming smile was in full flow.

The dance ended, watching from my vantage point I saw the various couples make their way back to their seats, men mainly on one side women on the other. I couldn't see the dark one until suddenly she emerged alone at the entrance to the balcony and she resumed her seat. I got up and slowly walked over to her, sat down and said "If the band was playing anything other than a waltz, foxtrot or quickstep I would ask you to dance".

She turned a warm smile on to me and said in a beautiful welsh accent, "You must be some dancer then."

"Oh yes" I replied, "Victor Sylvester was one of my first students."

She laughed, "Who are you? I've not seen you here before."

My natural instincts to spin a romantic colourful picture of myself took some controlling, but I still had some time to live in Aberystwyth and she might help it become even more attractive.

"I'm living on a yacht in the harbour *My Amour* nice name!! We arrived last weekend and will be here for a month maybe."

"Why a month, what are you doing with it," she asked.

"We're carrying the flag of Aberystwyth round the Mediterranean."

"You're what?"

"I dunno, it seems a good idea. Does Aberystwyth have a flag?"

"You should ask the mayor," she said, "he might know, I believe he's a keen sailor"

"I might do that," I replied, "first find me a mayor."

"Are you serious?" she said.

"I guess there is a serious side to me but it may take some time to emerge, you see." *No stick to the truth boyo, there's a month to go.* "Are all Welsh people anti brit?"

"Well I'm not," she said. "Why do you ask that?"

"I've been in a couple of shops and as soon as I get in they start talking in Welsh even though they were speaking English as I entered."

"Why did you change the subject?" she asked,

"It's something that has worried me, I wondered if I was smelly or something."

"You are that" she said turning on that beautiful smile, "I could recommend a good soap."

"I think I am working on you," I said.

"I like your smile."

"What about my face?"

"I like that too. Can we dance a bit, you're not really Welsh are you?"

"Yes, well half and half."

I stood up and held out my hand which she took and we walked down the stairs to the dance floor, It was a waltz, I made a mental note to keep to 1 2 3 time. She slipped easily into my arms, as we were about to move I made to hold her close, I was firmly held at arms-length and she said, "Tell me what you really do".

I told her what I had been doing at Butlins adding a few romantic versions of stories and found it was no effort at all to talk to her. We finished the three waltz's, why are there always three numbers? Then we stood waiting for the next music, we danced for about a quarter of an hour and then wandered back up to the balcony, when we sat down, she said, "You must leave me now and dance with some of the younger girls."

"But I've no desire to do that, I haven't even noticed anyone else".

"If I dance and talk with you all evening it will get back and that's that."

"You're married and you're a nurse aren't you?"

"Right on both counts but please leave me. How did you know I was a nurse?"

"Not before you promise another dance, the last waltz preferably."

"I'll see" she said smiling again.

"I'll go walk up and down for an hour, what time does it finish here?" I asked "Midnight?"

"No" she said, "11.30 and I have to leave at 11.15."

"Have you far to go, how do you get home?"

"I walk and it's not far, I live near the church."

"Does your husband meet you?"

"No he's away all week."

"Can I see you home if I'm not allowed any more dances." I felt the seriousness showing in my face, hey come on I've only known her for half an hour, "Do you really want me to go?"

"Yes you must, if you were outside at 11.15 up the street to the left I'll walk past you and you can follow but keep a distance between us."

"Are you serious" I asked, eagerness lighting up my face.

"Yes if you go now". I slowly got up, *what the hell, I'll buy a coffee or tea.*

I didn't feel like starting any more conversations. I said goodbye making a show of leaving and went down to the gents then on my way to the tea bar Tony appeared, large as life with his beauty in tow. "Where have you been?" he shouted above the noise of the band, "I haven't seen you all night, look what I've found, we're nearly engaged". He gave her his widest smile and winked at her. Tony's wink was legend. I first noticed it when he was photographing the proceedings at the Beauty Queen, Miss Britain contest at Butlins. He was doing his first season at Skeggy, as press photographer and many of his pictures found their way into the now defunct News Chronicle, which ran a full centre page of pictures each day during the summer season from the Butlins Holiday Camps. I remember only too well a publicity shot of me reading an elephants foot in one newspaper.

It was the beginning of the season, I was one of the judges along with Dave Allen, Norman someone our cricket coach and Joe Daniels, the band leader. Rows of pretty, not so pretty and a few almost ugly girls were persuaded to enter by the redcoats or their boyfriends of the week, They paraded in front of us judges, whilst whistles from the packed audience around the main swimming pool where it was held each week were intended to support them. Gradually the girls were whittled down to a manageable six finalists, who all stood in a row in front of us, the clever ones fixing on a judge and carefully letting their left knee rest belatedly over their right. I believe this is to either appear thinner, sexier, or is nervousness covering as much of one thigh as they can. In fact it's fairly difficult to capture in words what a parade of 'personal attributes' does, however at this point I was scratching my 'Palmists Beard' for effect of deep concentration, Tony was introduced as the photographer and he swung into action loudly telling the last girls to concentrate on him and his 'magic eye'. He peered through his lens, focused it presumably, then lowered the camera a bit and gave them the most marvellous wink. His complete face was given over to this wink. He was a good six feet tall, broad, well built, marvellous smile, white teeth, and the wink. I believe that the judges, the potential beauty queens, and about 1,000 campers were captivated by the wink.

Tony photographed each one then stepped back as we made our final judgement and the three who had made it were called in reverse order. The winner a stunning girl went on to the finals in London and was third in the country. Perhaps the wink had given her confidence.

I found during my years at Butlins that the winners were often very generous girls who would gladly be pliable to judges if the situation demanded it.

Back to the present.

Tony shouted, "Come and meet Annette's friend she's waiting for her palm to be read."

"I was just going for a coffee or tea, I suppose we can't get a drink here can we?"

"Not likely" said Annette, "why don't you introduce us Tony."

"I've told you all about him," grumbled Tony, but "Annette, Prof."

I said "Hello." She was certainly a beauty, long brunette hair, light brown eyes beautiful big lips and a figure that would do an hour glass justice.

"Its Brian," she said with emphasis on the *ian* bit. "Yes I guess although you can call me anytime", she smiled "next thing you'll be telling me you can put my name in lights."

"He's told you that one has he" I said, "I suppose his father is the electrician now."

"Come off it prof" this from Tony, "Lets go meet Gaye."

"Ok Tony, but I have a church to go to at 11.15."

"Tell me another, anyway the service will be over by then, or is it a candlelight ceremony?" he laughed "You know he gets inspiration from above Annette, some of the campers thought he was all powerful, particularly the one that got her foot caught in his cooking utensils". He doubled up at his own humour and gave me the wink.

I had told him of one particularly active night in my caravan with a very tall girl named Valerie who had somehow got her foot caught in my eating utensils which were neatly held up against the wall of the van by a device rather like a hinged carrier alongside the bed and the small sink, Knives forks spoons and etc's suddenly rained down on my unprotected backside, bringing with them a sharp reminder of another kind of satisfaction.

We walked through to meet Gaye. I sat down beside her and the four of us chatted but my mind was elsewhere and it wasn't long before 11 o'clock arrived and I slowly made my way to the door, walked out and went round the building before eventually settling on a rail that supported a variety of roses I guessed as one gave me a tear at my wrist.

If I was a smoker I would casually light up I thought, flip the match or better still roll my own. It wasn't long before I saw her approach and walk fairly quickly past not looking at me. I followed at a discreet distance perhaps some twenty yards or so. We wound our way through two dimly lit streets until we turned a corner and there was the church in front of me, It had a small arched building at its entrance opening directly onto the street, she went into the arch and I followed, when I got in it was quite dark and I could just make out where she was sitting on one of the benches that ran along each wall.

I was now totally intrigued and somewhat excited anticipating whatever was to be.

"This beats any hotel room." I said.

"Don't be overconfident" she says, "I thought we could at least be alone and free to talk here."

"I'm not much good at that after 11," I said.

"Come now" she said, "tell me one thing honestly, do you care who it is?"

"There are times when I am led into romantic situations without a thought for the consequences, other times I need a good push to get any inspiration, and times like now when I really am intrigued and smitten."

"Smitten with what?" she asked

"Well I enjoyed your company, talking with you at the dance and I would have really enjoyed spending the whole evening with you, we seemed to get along very easily, but, as I was following you through the streets, wondering if an angry husband would leap out at me, it hit me like a ton of bricks, I don't even know your name, you know mine, cos I mentioned it through my palm reading."

"You realise I can't see you anymore after tonight, I know you live on a boat and I realise how easy it would be for me to come with you, but no doubt your friend will have girls with him there. I watched the two of you in the dance hall and you obviously share a lot."

"We were not that close at Butlins, we played poker occasionally together and we met at many of the events there but we have only grown close through this adventure."

I moved a little closer and took both her hands in mine, "I would love to kiss those beautiful lips".

"You don't even know my name, how could you kiss a stranger?" she smiled

I left the arch some half hour later, pleading to see her again. Yes she often went to the Wednesday dances, but only if her husband was away, he wasn't into dancing. I let her walk on before I went out onto the esplanade and walked back to the boat. I heard noises coming from Beth's room and Tony's laughter as I crawled into bed.

CHAPTER 2

The Dixon's came every weekend with more provisions, paraffin, powdered milk, dried fruit. Mrs Dixon had given a great deal of thought to our requirements and we had enough to last several weeks. Our days were matched to the tides, when it went out we scraped at the hull and as we finished each side we would then paint it with the special sealant.

The great day approached, Bill took us all out each weekend to learn more about sailing and how to handle the boat. We decided that the first leg of our journey would be to Fishguard and tie up there. That would be good practice. Then the next leg would be to one of the Cornwall ports. The boat under full sail would really rattle along even though she was stuffed with provisions and her eight foot draught kept her on a pretty even keel even under windy conditions.

The mayor of Aberystwyth came down to see us all on the Saturday morning before our trip. He presented Bill Dixon with the flag of the town and we dutifully agreed that we would proudly fly it through the med. It was all arranged, we were to leave the following Thursday morning, at about 7am, when the tide was at its highest. There would be a small band to play us out.

This was excitement, I bought some more films for my Rollieflex. Tony did too, he had three cameras. He sold his motor bike to a local dealer and complained bitterly on the price he received.

The last few days were spent checking and rechecking all our provisions, we drank in the local pub with Bill Lucas each evening and he was really worried for our future, we were too excited to even think of anything going wrong.

My alarm clock buzzed, it was 6.30, breakfast time, I shook Tony who was in the land of dreams, we washed in our little basin, then surfaced and met Bill Dixon who was already in the cabin heating water for tea. Beth sleepily spilt out of her room and said she would make the toast and boiled eggs. Our demeanour was of controlled excitement, the anticipation of setting off to a band and official support for our venture was beyond our dreams. The sun was just climbing over the hills to the east of us and it looked like it would be the perfect day for a cruise.

As we were finishing our breakfast, Mrs Dixon hadn't appeared yet, we heard a call from the quayside, it was Bill Lucas. "Are you up? The Mayor and the band are just arriving."

We scrambled out of the cabin, Mr Dixon went to call Mrs Dixon. We lined up on deck and Bill came down and shook our hands, he gave both Tony and me a hug, "Its been great fun," he said, "take care and remember all the things I have shown you, this is a great boat and the eight foot draught should see you alright in all conditions."

Mrs Dixon appeared just as the Mayor looked over the quayside and wished us all the good fortune in the world, the band started playing something I vaguely recognised and Bill untied the rope aft, pushed us out from the quayside and then went forward to untie the other rope. Mr Dixon had started the two engines, he gave a toot on our horn and we set off slowly through the narrow channel out to sea. Bill Lucas was waving, the band was playing and the Mayor gave us an embarrassed salute.

It was lovely, there was hardly any wind, the sea was calm, the sun was climbing and we made steady progress, we had the main sail out and, Ol' man Dixon, as Tony and I referred to him when out of earshot, was in control. I sat up on deck with Tony and we watched Aberystwyth slowly fade in the distance. Mrs Dixon appeared in the cabin and offered tea or coffee and within very little time it seemed we were offshore Fishguard, in fact it was about 11.45. Bill Dixon called us into the cabin and suggested that as it was so calm and easy, why not go straight on to Penzance, we both agreed. We planned how we would do the watches during the night, two hours on, four off, for the men.

We took turns through the afternoon with steering the boat, we just used the sail and she seemed very happy, the wind was gentle and coming in from the west. Later in the afternoon as Tony relieved me with the tiller, I went and sat up front and just looked at the sea as it swept past our bow, the waves were still small just a gentle swell but it did seem to be getting a little darker and had an oily look to it.

Tony suddenly shouted "Hey, there's an island ahead of us."

I had an AA map in my file and went to look at it, Mr Dixon had acquired maps of the med but had forgotten to do the same for the Welsh coast. I looked at the map, it was Ramsay Island, a bird sanctuary, and it had Ramsay sound about fifty yards wide.

"What shall we do?" asks Tony?

"I think its safer to go round outside it," Bill Dixon suggested.

Tony aimed the boat out to sea a bit. "Its not responding too well," he said "shall we start the engines as well?"

Bill started both engines and they responded immediately. As we started rounding the island getting further away from land, the wind increased and the waves grew to something like six feet, and turned even darker, they were beginning to rush past us.

Ol' man Dixon, had recently had coronary problems and had been told not to overexert himself. Beth had told us this worrying news as we had sat in the morning sunshine on our way to Fishguard. He took over the tiller and Tony and I went on deck to take down the sail, this got a bit out of hand, the wind creating great difficulty. We eventually got it down after a lot of flapping, with me hanging on to the boom and wrapping it around its wooden splice. It was also getting a bit colder and the day was closing in.

Both our engines were beating away, Mrs Dixon disappeared into her room and the four of us sat in the cabin watching darkness fall and the sea picking up as the wind increased. We were somewhat concerned and not looking forward to a night in strange surroundings, total darkness, no radio and not a great deal of experience to call upon from any of us. Why had we not asked for a weather forecast when we were outside Fishguard, I thought, we could have been happily tied up there and enjoying an evening in the town.

Beth announced she would make a simple dinner, and started getting out all the necessary provisions and pans. I went below to our bedroom and hunted through my things for some warmer clothing, Bill Dixon set course south west and we ploughed on in darkness.

We had our meal, Beth took some to her mother who apparently was not feeling too well and was staying in her room. Mr Dixon would do the first two hours, and I would follow him from ten to midnight, Beth and Tony played cards. Bill joined his wife and had some sleep we presumed. I just kept the boat heading southwest and watched Tony and Beth. It was Thursday, the day we had set off in high hopes and here we were already tired and dispirited, watching a storm gather momentum. I sent Tony down to the engine room to oil the drives on both engines. Our engines had to be oiled regularly when being used. My eyes were beginning to ache from staring into nothingness.

Midnight arrived and I handed over to Tony. Beth was making some Horlicks for them but I turned down the offer, I needed sleep and crept down below. I only had four hours before I would be up again.

I immediately went to sleep, the boat was rolling a bit and I think it helped me drop off. I awoke with a start as Mr Dixon was knocking on the door and he said that the drives on both engines had ceased. Apparently Tony and Beth had been up together and whatever had happened, it had taken his mind off the fact that the engines needed oiling regularly, and he had forgotten. It was pitch black, the wind was whistling and sighing through the various ropes on the boat, the enormity of what had happened sunk in, we were without power, our sail could not be used and we were in the middle of an ever increasing storm. Where were we? Mr Dixon had bought a D.F. direction finder, that was our sole method of determining our position, he laid the equipment out on the table in the cabin, we had my torch and he judged that we were somewhere off Lundy Isle and we were drifting. He told Tony to keep the boat heading into the wind, we were climbing the waves and at the top dipping with a suddenness that was a bit frightening.

The three of us, all very tired and somewhat scared bolstered each other up, we would fire off distress signals when daylight came Beth was to make distress flags that could pulled to the top of the mast, we shouldn't be too far from Lundy and it was a busy channel so there should be plenty of traffic to help us.

Dawn came, none of us had had any more sleep, we both sent Tony off to bed, he had been up all night and so upset at what he had done that he just kept apologising. The storm was increasing, we were now staring out at enormous waves that towered over us, the boat would slide up them and then crash down the other side. The wind was blowing constant spray, each wave top would have a great stream of spray spreading out and some washed over the boat and began to drip into the cabin. It was important to keep the boat heading into the storm.

Mr Dixon decided he would fire off a couple of distress rockets, he put on his waterproof gear, stood by the cabin door and let off the first one which disappeared into the sky and was immediately blown back in the wind, at the same time another great wave washed over the prow of the boat and some of it poured into the cabin.. He hastily shut the door and then we heard a great crack from above us,

What could that be, maybe something blown over. No the mast, which was built through the boat, was cracked, it showed a bit beneath the deck where it entered the cabin. The crack seemed to be in the centre of the mast. Mr Dixon thought that it would not affect the boat in any way, it meant however that we would not be able to use the sail. How could we possibly consider getting outside and putting up a sail in a force ten gale. We were drifting and utterly helpless.

Beth got up and offered breakfast, neither Bill Dixon nor I were very hungry but she said we must eat. She made tea first, I was on the tiller and she handed me up a cup of tea, as I went to reach for it a huge wave hit us and I was thrown right over the wheel, and dropped the tea over Beth. Luckily she had on some thick clothes. It didn't touch her face or any exposed skin but she was soaked down her front. She started to cry more with fright than pain and Bill comforted her.

"What are we going to do?" she asked.

"I want you to make some distress flags that we can fly" he said, "it will keep your mind away from the storm and be helpful."

She made some toast and marmalade, then dutifully went off to see if her mother wanted any, but the answer was no, she was feeling very seasick and was beginning to slide back and forth in her bunk as the sea tossed the boat around.

We spent the day at the mercy of the storm, we somehow kept her head into the wind but during the late afternoon we could just make out some rocks a few hundred yards away.

"I think that's Lundy," said Mr Dixon. "I will fire another distress signal."

"No let me", I said, "When she's finished them I will also fix Beth's distress flags to the mast ropes and pull them up to the top of it".

Tony held the tiller and I got into Mr Dixon's wet gear, I had not given a thought to buying my own, nor had any of the Dixon's suggested that I might need anything for wet weather. Oh planning I thought.

I tied Beth's distress flags to the mast rope pulled it up as the others stood staring out of the cabin, it immediately wrapped itself around the rope and virtually disappeared. I fired off the distress signal, it swerved its way up into the clouds and disappeared. We continued to drift slowly past the rocks, some two hundred yards away and also covered in spray. It must be Lundy we all assumed. This means we are going up the Bristol channel. We all perked up, we must be seen, there must be other ships in the channel, gradually we stopped drifting and seemed to be stationary, all the time riding up enormous waves and we noticed we were beginning to take water, there was some rolling around the base of the hold. Where could that have come from?

"We must jettison most of our provisions and paraffin," said Mr Dixon, "we have to lose weight."

We started to throw things over the side, most of the things we had lovingly stowed away disappeared into the sea. Then we noticed that we were drifting back past the island, Lundy, but going the other direction. We were obviously in the Bristol channel and were being affected by the tides. We were being washed out towards the Irish Sea.

We somehow held out through the day, the storm continued and if anything intensified, we were beginning to roll with the boat, really getting our sea legs, and we started baling out as we were definitely taking water from somewhere. We had prised up a floor board and dipped in our bucket and handed the water up from one to the other. In a short time we had removed most of the water. We now had Mrs Dixon's battery powered light hanging in the cabin, we had not seen anything of her all day, and darkness came. With it a certainty that our condition was pretty desperate, the only saving grace was that *My Amour* seemed to be able to keep afloat and ride the waves.

We spent the day baling out keeping our head into the storm coming from the west, we never saw Lundy again all day, we were all exhausted but we somehow managed to eat a bit sleep a bit and generally keep our spirits up with the hope that we would either get rescued or get back up the Bristol channel to safety.

Friday night; this was our second night at sea. The storm was still raging. What were our prospects? I said I will see if I can free the drives on the engines in the morning, I had spent a little time when in my teens as a trainee fitter in Gainsborough and I thought I would have a go at it. We took turns at keeping the boat into the teeth of the storm through the night. We all hung around a while after our shift had finished, it was the company that kept our thoughts positive.

Dawn broke, the sea was still enormous, the spray was if anything more insidious than the previous days, I got the tool set out after Beth had made some toast and coffee, Tony was on the tiller and Bill Dixon was comforting his wife who had still not emerged at all during the trip.

I went down into the engine room – hardly an engine room it was tiny and difficult to move in – just a small area with very little space and two whacking great engines lying totally still. I took off the cowling on the nearest engine, the drive rod was covered in burrs and solid. I somehow managed to free it and started to file off the burrs. I was very short of air, the boat was continually rocking and plunging and it took me two hours of painful work to get the drive rod free. I oiled the connecting rod and managed to refit it then I tightened all the bolts and nuts and checked that all was tight. It was time to try again and I kicked the starter, on the second kick the engine gave a growl and turned over, within a few seconds it was thumping happily away and we had power. I shouted up to the others that I had it working, but the wind was too strong for them to hear me. I squeezed out of the engine room flushed with success, as I did so Beth appeared above the entrance, hanging on to the hand rail and as a wave hit the boat she slipped and poured hot cocoa over me, luckily it only went over my clothes and I felt a soggy warmth, she cried out in fright but I was ok, I hauled myself along the deck hanging on grimly, one minute almost touching the water the next we would be riding high at the top of a giant wave. She followed me. I staggered in to the cabin. "I've started one of the engines."

Tony burst into tears and threw his arms around me.

Bill Dixon had heard the engine He came rushing up from his room and congratulated me. I was covered in oil, my clothes were wet through from the cocoa and rain but I didn't care. I suggested we head for Bude Bay which was alongside Lundy, beach the boat and dash for the shore. Mr Dixon said no, he said he was heading in the direction of the Bristol channel, we would negotiate that and get ashore that way. He took over the tiller. Tony and I went down to our cabin and I said "I don't believe it, we are heading out to sea."

Tony burst into tears again and I said lets go up and persuade him to turn the other way. We went up and both decided to stand outside the cabin hanging on to whatever was stable, we faced into the storm and we commiserated with each other, it had been a good idea but we should never have tried to get too far the first day. Whilst we were standing there watching the boat crawl crabwise up yet another huge wave I suddenly shouted. "Look Tony!" Ahead of us was a huge grey ship and it was signalling to us. I rushed into the cabin grabbed my torch, wedged myself outside the door and my boy scout training manual stood me in good stead, looking down at the book I started to spell out. Please signal slowly, looked up and the ship had disappeared in the mist and spray.

Tony, face alight with excitement said yes there was definitely a huge ship there, Suddenly alongside us was the ship, one moment we were looking at rust on its hull, the next minute we were level with their deck as we were tossed about on the huge waves.

"Are you alright *My Amour*?" shouted a voice from a loud hailer.

Bill Dixon came out of the cabin with our hailer and shouted "We have women on board, we're in trouble."

The voice shouted back "We will send our sea boat and take them off, what do you want to do?"

"We have two women but us three men will stay on board, can you tow us in to Bristol?"

"No but we can take to Milford Haven."

Then began a wonderful sequence of events. On the deck of the ship, a cruiser, were several ratings, some were throwing up over the rail on which they were gripping, the voice on the loud hailer we discovered was the bosun, *HMS Salisbury*, our saviour, was from Portsmouth; it had brought out several new ratings and they were being given a taste of really bad weather, their induction to the sea.

The cruiser had been using us as radar target practice all morning, the Captain thought we might well be a fishing smack. Fishermen go out in all weather. But, and this was the good news, they had come to look at us before they set off to Milford Haven. Just to make sure.

A long boat being crewed by about twelve ratings came out from *HMS Salisbury*, they drew up alongside us, rocking with the huge waves, they manoeuvred their boat so that we both climbed waves in parallel, Beth came out of her cabin and so did Mrs Dixon, who was looking totally green and very shaky. We had not seen her for three days.

Two of the seamen had jumped onto our boat and they had blankets which they wrapped round the ladies, they lifted Mrs Dixon over the side and manhandled her into the front of their boat. Beth was quickly pulled down and seated at the rear. Then they set off riding the waves and we watched them anxiously as they tipped and turned with the waves, unseen hands pulled them into their ship and took the two ladies on board.

Bill Dixon said "I hope you don't mind staying on board boys but I don't want them to claim my boat as salvage. They will tow us into Milford Haven."

We were overjoyed to be rescued. The loud hailer said "Either get into the cabin or lie beneath the gunwales."

Tony went into the cabin with Mr Dixon who was still holding her into the wind and I laid beneath the gunwales, There was a twanging and an arrow swung over our boat tied to a small rope.

"Pull it in" shouted the bosun. I balanced as best as I could and started to haul the rope in, it was knotted to a sizeable hawser and when I had about ten yards of it on board the bosun told me to tie it forward, which I did.

I struggled back to the cabin and watch *HMS Salisbury* start off, the rope swished out of the sea and suddenly we were travelling about ten knots, we had only just started to really slip though the water, jumping over the crest of the waves when the hawser unhooked at their end. We immediately stopped and Mr Dixon turned her into the wind again.

The Cruiser reversed until it towered over us again for a few seconds and then we were lifted right up above it. The bosun by now was leaning over his rail above us and demanded that we pull in the hawser onto our boat. He shouted it had come undone at their end ... as if we didn't know. I went cautiously forward and started to pull in this thick rope, as *My Amour* rolled to the left I would pull in a yard or so, she would then straighten up and two feet would go back in the sea. I kept at it for what seemed hours and eventually our boat seemed to be entirely covered in piled hawser and I reached the flawed piece that had snapped at their end.

He shouted on his hailer. "Lay beneath the gunwales," which I did. *Twang* another arrow sliced through the hawser. It had a small rope attached. "Tie it safely to the end" he shouted. Tony came forward and tied it while I lay there covered in thick wet hawser.

The bosun gave the order to pull in the hawser. It started and Tony's knot came undone. The bosun called him every name under the sun and swore at him for some time without using the same swear words twice. Tony's face crumpled and tears were very near the surface. "Pull it back on again," the bosun shouted.

We both pulled it this time and when we had were told to lie down again. *Twang* I was getting used to the arrow by now and said. "Hang on Tony I learnt about knots in the scouts." I tied a double bowline and the order went out to pull it in, after some few minutes they had the hawser. It was tied and we again set off for Milford Haven, we positively skipped over the crest of waves as they went at about 12-15 knots; they wanted to get us in before dark.

After some time of a frightening journey, watching the hawser bury itself in the waves then suddenly appearing again leaping into the air, tightening up, and we would lurch along behind the cruiser, we entered much calmer water and towering on either side of us were the hills of Milford Haven. We went up the estuary and after some time the cruiser slowed right down and the bosun informed us that he was handing us over to the port authorities and we were to be taken the rest of the way by a tug which was standing by.

We gave the crew a cheer the three of us, they were all heroes as far as I was concerned, we wallowed in the swell that was running in the estuary and as it was getting dark a tug appeared alongside us, one of the crew jumped on board our boat and tied a hawser to us. They set off at a good pace and Tony and I were sitting on the deck when I noticed that their towing rope was across our bows and we were leaning well over and water was beginning to splash over the side and into our boat. I shouted at them but they were out of earshot, and I said to Tony "We've been through all this and we are about to sink here, we must put our life jackets on."

He burst into tears again. Incredibly, none of us had worn a lifejacket throughout the three days that we had been exposed to some of the worst weather and conditions the Welsh coast had seen for many years. I rushed to the cabin, Mr Dixon was getting very upset trying to right the boat, I grabbed my torch and started flashing at the tug finally the message got through and they stopped and came right alongside and tied us tightly to them.

Tony and I sat on the deck comforting each other. "Tony," I said "We have just been through the most amazing experience and neither of us took any pictures of it, they would have been priceless."

Tony smiled, "Were you thinking of photographs at the time? I wasn't, I was absolutely terrified and although I didn't say it to you, I thought we'd had it."

I nodded and we sat silently as we approached dry land. We were brought up to the quayside. There were television cameras, pressmen and several people who had been following our plight for some time. Apparently Bill

Lucas had warned the coastguards down the west coast of our journey and as the weather had turned sour they had been broadcasting on the radio for our boat. As we hadn't got a radio we had been completely out of touch.

I found that I was staggering around on dry land, we were filmed and photographed for some minutes Mr Dixon gave interviews and queried as to the whereabouts of the ladies?

"You had women on board too, where are they."

"Yes," Bill said.

"Where are they?"

A message got through they had been taken to the Golden Lion pub/inn where we were to spend the night, we were also invited to a party on board *HMS Salisbury* the next lunch time.

For many days after our rescue whenever I stood on a wooden floor I would start to roll about. But we went to *HMS Salisbury* and were given a royal welcome. The Captain was the most cheerful man and he was fascinated by our complete lack of knowledge about anything concerning the sea and sailing, and as we left the cruiser each of us were given a bottle of rum and we left with his words ringing in our ears.

"You were lucky but I wouldn't try again for a while. Thank your draft."

I went back to the Lion with Tony and the Dixon's. *My Amour* had been left lying on her side quite near to where we had stepped ashore, she looked extremely sad and knocked about. Mr Dixon said he would try to get her made shipshape but would not be sailing again. I think Mrs Dixon had had some words about that.

I laid on my bed in the pub and read a magazine called, *The Stage*, that had been left outside my room. There were several articles about the theatre and shows and also an advert for men with red beards. Gillette were looking for men with red beards for a series of photographic adverts. I had a red beard.

The next day Bill Dixon gave both Tony and me £35 each, we had breakfast together in the pub and we talked of our experience. We all agreed that we had been very foolish to attempt to take on the sea and perhaps we should stick to dry land in future. We nevertheless had made strong ties through our adversity and we were quite sorry to have to say goodbye.

Tony and I caught a bus to London and we said a fond farewell to Beth and promised to keep in touch. Tony went on to Chichester but I went to the RAFFA club near Marble Arch and the next day presented myself at the address given for the Gillette advert. It was in St Martins Lane, I went in my sandals, trousers cut off at the knee and a duffle coat that had seen better days. It had been hanging in a boat for a while and needed a clean. There were several other young men mainly in suits and quite smart, but we all had something in common, reddish beards.

I asked a young girl at reception what I had to do.
She said "Did your agent send you?"

"Agent?" I asked, "I saw this ad in the stage, it said you were holding interviews yesterday and today. I've just come from Milford Haven and have been lost at sea for nearly a week."

She smiled, "Oh yes, what's your name?"

"Brian Bada" I said.

"I will see if I can arrange an audition".

I was eventually the last one to be invited to go into the casting room by the pretty secretary, I shambled in and sitting behind a long table were two men and a woman, virtually in one voice they said "that's the one."

I was amazed, then they asked me what experience I had in front of the camera. I briefly told them that I had just finished a season with Butlins. I was a personality and palm reader, I was used to being photographed with 'Glamourous Grannies', 'Miss Englands', Nobbly knees winners, and reading elephants feet, which amused them, and I was handling myself. I didn't have an agent. Just back from being lost at sea for four days…

I thought that might have got some recognition but it was obviously late and they were longing for their gin and tonics. "Give all your details address etc., to the secretary and she will inform you when we need you."

"Fee" I asked, "how will I be paid"?

"She will send all you need to know, in the next few days."

I did a series of 'shoots' for Gillette, with several stills.

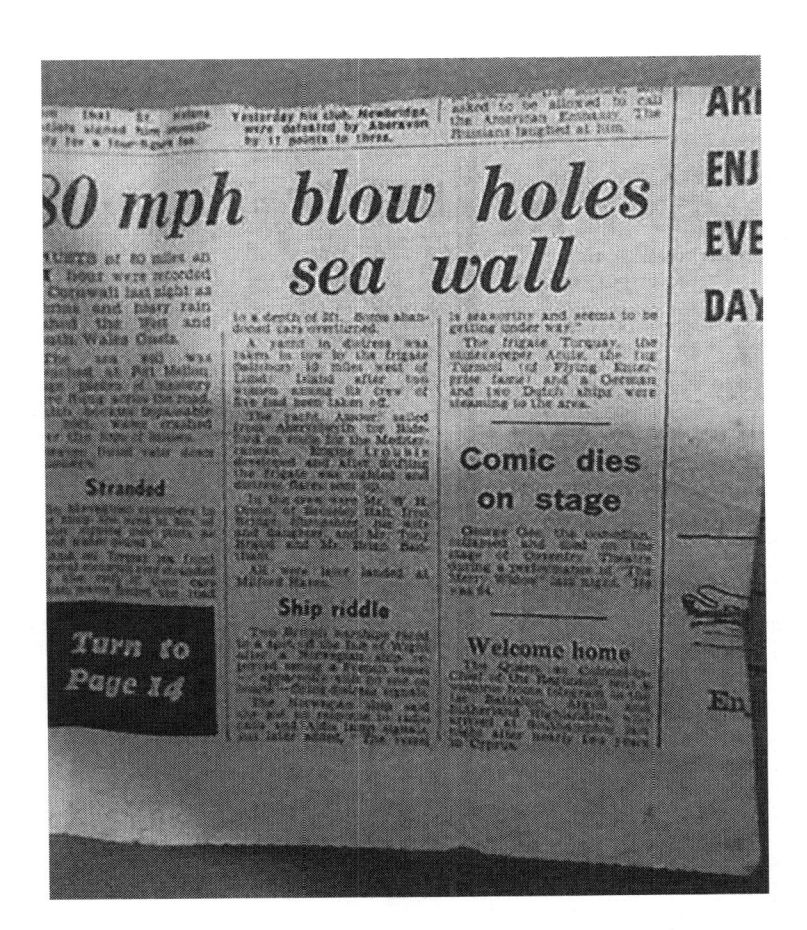

Newspaper reports of the bad weather and
our ill-fated cruise

Yacht party will fly to Vienna — to forget

STORM-HIT FAMILY ABANDON CRUISE

WESTERN MAIL REPORTER

FIVE holidaymakers who nearly lost their lives in storm-tossed waters off the Welsh coast on Saturday have cancelled their six-month Mediterranean cruise. Now, thankful to be alive, they will holiday in Vienna—flying out by plane.

Islanders may learn Russian

CAR STRIKE NEWLYWEDS 'VERY UPSET'

SHE PUTS HER ART BEFORE HEART

'Frightened'

Trujillo calls up troops

Towed in

Iron and steel output up

'Magnificent'

CHAPTER 3

I was born in Caston Norfolk on the 26th of June 1932 to a loving mum and dad. Mum owned the village store, Dad had a smallholding farm. I had one brother – Roy, four years older than me.

Caston has been and still is a farming village, it was initially a forested area and part of Wayland Wood, of *Babes in the Wood* Fame. I did a bit of research into my village when at Thetford Grammar School and it is not known exactly when the settlement of Caston was organised into a manor, but it seems to have been prior to the Norman Conquest of 1066. The de Caston family began their tenure of the manor, taking their surname from the name of the village, they were a prominent family in Norfolk holding a number of manors. Caston has been derived from Catt's Tun, Catt being a Scandinavian name and tunn an Anglo-Saxon word which originally meant fence or an enclosure and evolved to be a settlement of huts.

My mother's shop, 'Banhams General Stores', was very successful and sold everything it was possible to provide – even in the war years.

My father's small farm had some cows and calves, it provided fresh vegetables, and we also had a huge orchard which boasted apple trees with the splendid names of Doctor Brown, Newton Wonders, Beauty of Bath, Cox's

Orange Pippin, Russets *ugh urgh*, pears, plums and a walnut tree. The big garden had soft fruit. As a penance for something I had done, I can't remember what, one year I was made to gather the apples from our two Russett apple trees. For two days I collected the rough rough skin of them and seventy years later I still shudder at the thought of anything rough, in fact if I should touch a rough elbow, or when caressing a foot, if I feel any roughness, waves of horror go through to my sensitive brain. Large parts of the orchard were wired off with netting so our hens could live in there without being grabbed by foxes and I loved going into the pen and digging up some of the earth, surrounded by cackling hens waiting to grab any worms that appeared.

Our walnut tree was famous in the village as it often had a resident nightingale which would sing through the summer evenings. Many a night I would crawl up to my bedroom window to listen to the most beautiful song echoing round the village. It was a family joke that my brother often found me asleep crunched up with Smut, my cat without a tail, purring contentedly in my lap. He would put me to bed and I would bore the family at breakfast trying to imitate the bird.

One of my earliest memories is when I was three years old and proudly riding my first three wheeled tricycle, alone for the first time, around the corner of our warehouse and *bang*! My big brother ran in to me on his two wheeled bike and his bell press cut the bottom of my nose where it joins my face. The next thing I knew I was sitting on the doctor's knee whilst he gave me a little stitch or two and my mother fussed over me.

I'm still a little bit conscious of that discrepancy even after years of scraping an electric shaver around my long shapely nose, although growing wrinkles and smiling crowfeet, have taken some of the shine from my beauty, the love of my life looks into my eyes and sees imperfection. I guess after years of sunbathing and turning brown, it has grown to be part of me anyway.

Our dog Bill was of a shaggy indeterminate breed with a permanent smile playing on his face. He and Smut used to vie for my attention and we perfected a little show for the family. I would hide in the outside loo or the garden shed, or in our enormous grapevine, when they found me it was to applause from all including my grandma. This was the signal for the start of the show. Bill raced down to the orchard and Smut hid in the garden flowers, I would whistle for Bill and he would come racing back and as he passed a clay wall, Smut would leap out onto his back and dig in to keep her position. It took me some time to realise that Bill must have had many claw marks but he didn't seem to mind. Smut had arrived in our family through her mother having a litter in the shop, under the clothes counter. I had stood on Smut's tail when she was very small and it had come off. I was so distraught that I showered all my love on to the tiny little kitten and several years later when I eventually left home she was the only thing I missed.

My uncle Reg lived with us and I had this sneaking feeling that my mum and dad were always a bit upset with him. He was my mothers' brother, a bachelor, with crisp curly hair, laughing eyes and was great fun. He taught me how to fart, not just little whispers but great big burly ones that would, as he said, 'echo round the village' He cycled off each day to work in Watton. I never knew at what. When the war came he went off never to return, apparently killed instantly at *El Alamein*, or so the notification said. My mother suffered terribly as she adored Reg – as we all did. She also lost a brother, Jack, in the first world war.

I joined the boy scouts and quite liked our assistant scout master until I heard he been seen knitting in bed, that put me off a bit, but I nevertheless went to the camps and eventually became the leader of the Lion Pack. I achieved some notoriety on one weekend camp as I had stood in a nest of vipers and my reaction was so startled and violent that I kicked out at them and one sailed over a group that was about to go into the woods in search of anything unusual. To see me whacking another with my scouts stick put me in the cowboy that 'shoots a rattler' fame. I never let on how scared I was.

One winter afternoon our scoutmaster's wife was cycling through the village when there was snow on the ground. I hastily grabbed a handful and threw it at her. I missed but she swerved and came a cropper, so I ran home and hid in the outside lavatory until I heard my mother calling me to come and apologise as she was there in the shop. Eventually I shuffled in and said "but I missed". This didn't go down too well, but it didn't seem fair at the time.

We lived opposite the bakers, they had a van and we had a car. In the summer months we took turns in using our transport to share days and picnics at Hunstanton and Wells where we would troll for cockles whelks and mussels, paddle and generally enjoy almost total isolation at the seaside.

I went to local village school which I enjoyed – certainly I enjoyed Pearls little fuzzy bit when we sat at the back of the class, Pearl being the bakers daughter and we took turns peering at our private parts.

The war had started. I remember a man in uniform arriving one day with another very seedy looking man who brought several boxes into the village classroom, they were gas masks. Unfortunately there were not enough for us all to have one so we took turns in having them hanging round our necks, sometimes for three or four days. We also had to help put up gummed sticky paper on all the school windows to protect them from any blast of bombs.

Some cockneys arrived in the village from Hackney, somewhere in London. We knew they were cockneys because they were very proud of it. They didn't have much idea of country life as they would beat a rabbit to death with sticks, whereas we would stretch their necks and kill them that way.

We had an army training ground at Doddington, quite close to Caston and one day the village was full of soldiers on manoeuvres and a Bren Gun Carrier crashed through and wrecked the railings of the school. This caused a great deal of excitement and we all stood around for some time just looking at it as they backed out from the railings and tried to straighten them. I seem to recall that country life entailed a great deal of standing around looking at something of interest. The war gave us plenty of that with the odd land mine which would give us good reason to stand and stare at the large hole left in the ground. "That's a hole made by a land mine" "Oh Yeah" several minutes would pass whilst we looked. "That's a big hole, must have been a big land mine" "Yeah" several more minutes would pass. In fact Norfolk people can stand without saying anything for a long time.

We also had, next door to the baker, a blacksmith, where we could watch him shoeing horses. I never understood why a horse stood patiently as he put a red hot shoe on its foot, steam escaping round the shoe, and he then hammered it in and bent the nails over the hoof.

We, my dad, had two horses – Prince and Tom. They lived in the lower meadow and most days I would get to the gate and whistle them and they would dutifully trot over and take the carrot or sugar lump I offered. I loved Tom, he would let me ride bareback and he could jump a bit. Prince was a solid horse very good with the plough and rake for the hard work in the fields.

In our village life was pretty simple, our one big social event was a fish and chip van that came round every Thursday night and stopped outside our shop. It was the local meeting place and all us young ones ran round in circles.

In the winter bat catching was a great pastime, but pretty frightening. I hated it yet was thrilled to do it. We had this technique that I learned from my brother, we would all bring our stiff garden brooms out and let the bats impale themselves as we waved them about over our heads, we could then study them by torchlight. Nasty little things made my flesh creep.

Christmas was a time when I really enjoyed our family. Dads sister, Aunt Alice and her family, either came to us or we to them on Christmas day. We would play games, Postman's Knock, or my favourite, Pin the Tail on the Donkey, which meant being blindfolded then spun around then trying to pin the long tail onto the donkey which was stuck on a large board. Cousin Sam had designed the donkey, I loved it and would play for hours.

The war had been going on for some time but we were not too exposed to it. We would see Norwich in the distance sometimes lit up when bombing was taking place and the searchlights were weaving around in the sky.

My brother acquired the name 'Digger' as he had taken bets in the local pub *The Red Lion*. He had boasted of being able to dig a two acre field by hand in three days, over a weekend. He did but his hands were so blistered from handling the spade he couldn't even roll a cigarette. He was four years older than me and he and his friends would pass their spare time in a variety of ways, one being a walk right round the village. I would sometimes want to go with them but they would throw stones at me and drive me back to the protection of our shop wall.

I found that sport was natural for me and the large end wall of the shop would be my practice area for football. Initially I would kick the ball against it then as I got bigger I would head the ball for hours. I had several friends in the village and much of our time was taken up with football on Peak Vouts field, or cricket in the summer on Major Petry's meadow where the village played its cricket.

I had built a tree house in our orchard with some of my school friends, we used to sneak up it and puff away at a Willy Woodbine, slyly taken from my mums shop. I longed to be old enough to smoke, but I thank my brother for obliterating that desire. One day he and I decided to shoot some pigeons for us to eat and sell in the shop. We laid in a ditch on my dads' land, under a tree laden with ivy – pigeons would feast on ivy – and as they flew into the tree we would shoot them. We were both good shots, I had a four-ten and my brother a twelve bore. During the day he gave me a Craven A, Black Cat, to smoke. It made me sick for two days and I have only ever smoked once since then when I did a commercial for Guards Cigarettes.

My father belonged to a large family of cousins – the Banhams. All were farmers and owned land in and around our village. The family was an early co-operative, all of them helped with each others crops. The sugar beet was an early season job planting, weeding, spacing them – a country art form. To make certain the beet had every chance of growing we had a long handled hoe with a six inch blade and we would race across lines of small beetroot plants, *chop, chop, chop*, leaving one every six inches. When they were big enough to gather we would follow the horse – pulled beet – lifter and the back breaking work of pulling out two beet, knocking them together to get the earth off them, and laying them facing inwards towards another row also facing in. We would then 'top' them, taking off the leaves with a very sharp hook, and throwing them into heaps down the middle of the two lines. When enough were done we loaded them onto a horse drawn tumbril and made a huge heap by the gate entrance to the field, so they could eventually be transported to the refinery at Bury St Edmonds.

Muck spreading was fun, particularly if you were working in unison with a friend. Heaps of horse or other animal dung would be spaced in heaps in rows on a field and you 'spread it' by sweeping forkfuls in a half circle, gradually working your way down the line. The real art was to land a large lump on your friend's head who would be working the parallel line to you. When the muck was spread our horse Prince would rake it in.

I enjoyed seed spreading, you had a round tin tray with a handle which you would hold tightly to your body when full, and a thick supporting string which would go round your neck, then take large handfuls of seed and walk slowly in a line down the field spreading the seeds. At either end of the field would be sacks of more seeds. It was always very satisfying to see them start to shoot and then see how effective your spreading had been.

The corn was always interesting because as it grew taller the rabbits would feed on it. When the time came to cut it as the mower, pulled by our horse Prince, made inroads into the field, the rabbits, and if you were lucky, the odd hare would eventually make a dash for the hedge. There were always a few guns around to make sure we had some for cooking. Rabbits and pigeons were our staple diet during the war. To see the corn shaking as a rabbit ran towards you was very exciting, a bit like watching your float dip under the water, when fishing in the local pond.

Another big occasion was when the threshing machine visited the village, or 'Thrasher' as it was known in Norfolk. All the Banham farmers would arrange their time to suit the owners of the machine and they all helped each other. It would be puffed into the village behind its steam engine and placed alongside a corn stack, in turn an elevator would be placed behind the thrasher to carry the straw onto another stack. During the threshing process there were various tasks, loading on to the thrasher, bagging the corn and worst of all, chaff and colder. This meant being totally wrapped in overalls tied at the bottom and a scarf or damp handkerchief tied tightly around your neck and covering your mouth as the dust, dirt and filth all came out of that part of the machine and it had to be bagged.

Then you had the rats to contend with. It was a common sight to see huge rats leaping out of the stack as the sheaves were thrown up to the thrasher. On one occasion I was doing the dreaded chaff and colder and I had a tap on my shoulder, when I turned my head I was looking into the eyes of a huge rat. I threw myself to the ground and tried to hit it as I fell. I remember one local old man who had a wooden leg from the knee down, who was loading sheaves onto the machine suddenly started to beat his groin, apparently he had not tied his trousers and a rat had got up to his knee before he realised it and it had gone straight to his groin. I suppose it could be exciting if you like that sort of thing.

Gradually the combine harvesters and tractors made inroads into a country way of life that was always exciting for the kids because everyone in the village had an interest in how things were achieved.

We had a comfortable house alongside the more modern shop, some rambling storehouses behind the shop and a cool house which was built when I was nine years old, to keep the butter cheeses and other cooler produce in. I became my mum's hero for rigging up a wire through a series of little hooks to a bell which would ring in the storerooms if anyone entered the shop. We would keep all our gathered apples wrapped individually in old newspapers and my mum would sell them through the year.

One of our features was a well, we could draw our water which was very fresh to drink, and my mother kept her shop butter and anything else that had to kept cool in sometimes icy water which I loved cranking and pulling up. The well had a triangle top to it so that any rain water would be shelved to the outside and it was also covered with wire mesh to deter any creatures or animals from getting in to it.

Friday night was bath night for us all, in front of the fire, my dad would fill the tin bath with water heated on the hob and we would take turns to dip in.

My dad would go to the pub some evenings and often bring back Americans who were based at Watton Air Camp, just a mile away from us. When they arrived in the village life took on a new interest. We were suddenly overwhelmed with marching GI's *"Hup two three four, Hup two three four, we had a good home and we left, You're right, we had a good home and we left, You're right"*. They were very untidy marched out of step and sang a lot.

There were two that came regularly to our house, Jay and Joey, they both played guitars and they would go into our orchard and sing cowboy songs, always songs of great loneliness, I loved to hear them sing; I developed a love of western songs which I still have. A bit of yodelling was also great. One night Joey came alone – Jay had not come back from a mission, he went into the orchard and cried as he sang. All our family took him to our hearts. There was another American, Jerry that I really liked. He brought me Superman and Batman comics, invited me back to the camp to see the planes and they had parties for the local kids where ice cream would be served. There were painted balloons on the walls – I didn't realise they were painted 'johnnies', until some time later.

When my dad went to help out at uncle Arthur's farm I would often go with him and play with Emily and

Margaret, his daughters. Doctors was out favourite game and we would get onto the lawn under a blanket and I would have to inspect them. Emily used to quiver when I touched her and she encouraged me to pretend I had a stethoscope and listen to her heart, which I and she enjoyed.

Our village had some wonderful characters. Norfolk men seemed to acquire nicknames and the village was full of them. One character called 'Billy Bouncer' was about four foot nine inches tall and he had a nurse girlfriend that was over six feet tall, they would walk through the village, he with his arm around her leg as he couldn't reach her waist and he bounced along, hence the name, much to the delight of all. Sugar Bailey acquired his name through a love of anything sweet, and Stoat Breeze his because of his nose that really made him look like a stoat. Enid Savoury was another star and her brother Cecil caused some merriment.

We had a boy named Cyril who was a Down Syndrome and he loved joining in anything we did, he was always laughing and appeared happy. As most country folk know, if you catch a hen or chicken hold its head to the ground, best on a path or road, then draw a white chalk line straight from its beak the chicken seems to be paralysed and will stay there for some time. Cyril wanted to do this but we just encouraged him to crow like our cockerel which would make him happy. One day we got him to put his willy in a milk bottle and he then got an erection and was proudly walking around with it hanging in his front.

We had seen some parachutes come down in Peek Vouts meadow, apparently on manoeuvres, practicing from Watton airdrome, and we made a model for Cyril from sacks. We tied and strapped it on him then he climbed Peek Vouts tree and jumped off from about ten feet high, he plummeted down into the muddy ditch running beneath the tree and was up to his knees in mud laughing at us all. Shortly after this his mother came into the shop and told my mother that he was going to a special school with other similar children. We missed him.

One night we had some land mines dropped on the outskirts of the village and some of our shop windows were blown in and broken. We all used to sit under the table when the siren went except for my other granny who would only put her head under it. "if moi hids awrite then Oim orwright" She died during the war.

I had one distressing time on a particularly hot day when several of us had gone to a ballast pit, as they were called, to paddle and swim, for those that could. I was standing on the bank near the deep end when someone pushed me in, I didn't know who, and I remember sinking deep looking up at the surface which appeared green, from being deep down. I flapped my arms a bit and just broke the surface and then started going down again, panicking and sucking in water. Somehow I came up again and was just about to sink when my brother jumped in and dragged me out. Apparently they laid me on my side and pummelled me until I was sick and threw out a flood of water. It caused me to have a fear of water and even today I still do not like to be very far out of my depth.

I passed the 11 plus and went with my mother to Thetford Grammar School to meet the headmaster, an upright man with a little moustache. I hadn't realised the significance of my meeting and was my usual casual self, not too much bothered if I created an impression or not. My mother was a bit fed up with me after our interview saying that I hadn't tried. I remember being very taken with the fact that the girls school was immediately opposite, in fact the heads house ran alongside their school. I was a little bit interested in girls but I think only for comparison with Pearl.

I made the grade, I expect because my mother fitted me out with real clothes and I wore a cap for the first time. I had spent many years wearing a red beret which I loved and only took it off for bed and the very odd bath in front of the fire in our tin tub.

Going to grammar school took up a great deal of my time and I gradually drifted away from the basic life that I so enjoyed in the village. Each morning I would cycle to Stow Bedon, leave my bike beside the station and take the Swaffam to Thetford 'Crab & Winkle'. My bike was always there when I returned!

I saw one frightening attack one morning, as the train pulled into Wretham station, the stationmasters dog, an Alsatian, was trying to get to a female Alsatian that was peering out of the carriage window, probably on heat. The stationmaster tried to pull it back and it attacked him, luckily two soldiers jumped out and pulled it off him but he was bleeding quite badly down his right arm. It reminded me of an episode when with my father we were driving one of our sows to farmer Greens boar and passing Mr Kettles house. His Alsatian ran out and knocked me over, it was standing over me with its fangs bared when my dad leapt up behind it and tore its front legs apart killing it instantly. It gave me a deep fear of Alsatians to this day. Mr Kettle, who worked for Arthur Banham was most apologetic even though he had lost his dog.

We would all mix on the train but it took me some time to get relaxed with the girls. The girl's grammar at Thetford, next door to ours, had several girls that were collected from the various stations. We boys would throw remarks at them and they would suffer us fools splendidly and come back calling us nasty names. We all walked in a crocodile from the station to the school, which I didn't enjoy.

I enjoyed the challenge of grammar school after the very curtailed and limited teaching in the village, moving from subject to subject with different teachers and classrooms for the various lessons. I particularly liked the French class as our teacher, Miss Robinson used to sit on the front desk with her legs a little open and we would all rush to get the desk immediately in front of her. As I was one of the biggest in our class I was often rewarded by getting it and having the odd stolen look. It didn't improve my French but she frequently entered my dreams as a real beauty as I was getting towards manhood!!

I was enjoying school and the formal classes and I was doing well when my Mother died. She was thirty five and I was thirteen. Tragic. She had been ill for only a couple of weeks, had gone to her bed, with breast cancer I discovered later, and we had to keep the curtains drawn as the light affected her eyes. We would take turns in sitting with her. I would hold her hand so when she woke she had company.

When I wasn't with her I spent all my time in my workshop making model airplanes, Smut would keep me company. My Aunt Marian appeared and stayed in the village, a few days later I was in my workshop when she came in and hugged me and said "Come and see your mum."

I sensed things were desperate. I went into the bedroom and my dad was sitting beside the bed, red eyed and exhausted. She was asleep. I sat there for a while with them and she didn't wake up. I held her hand, it was warm and I kissed her and said I would go back to my workshop.

A little later my aunt came hugged me and told me my mum had died. I just stared at her and sat down on the floor, and she went to get my dad. He came with tears streaming down his lovely face, sat on the floor beside me and put his arm around me. We didn't say anything. After a while he asked if I was alright. I nodded but I couldn't cry. He went out and I suspected he was standing outside my door. I looked out and he was standing looking down towards the orchard, his ever faithful country flat hat on and tears streaming down his lovely homely face. I crept back into my workshop again and hugged Smut; we sat there for ages, until Aunt Marian called me in for tea. I'm sure the terrible news of uncle Reg being killed, which was a telegram in a brown envelope handed over to my mother by a man in army uniform, had given her such a shock she had developed a very serious breast cancer which apparently had rapidly spread.

The house was empty without my mother and for the first time in my life I experienced real loneliness. I couldn't face the funeral and spent the day and night with Mike one of my mates. I heard the church bell toll for her service and when they buried her, we dug Mike's garden and tried not to think of what was going on. My Dad, brother Roy, and Aunt Marian and most of the village walked behind the car with the coffin from our house to the church. He said as the cortege passed the green in the front of the church there were five American GI's there. They stood to attention and saluted my mother.

The shop had prospered under my mother and she had had a helper for some of the days, Joan, whose father ran the local bus service. When my mother was unable to work any more Joan's sister Norma also came in.

I sang in the church choir and I know my mum was very proud of that, she also arranged music lessons with a rather large fat lady who had an odd smell. My mother had an organ which I would practice on but when she died I gave up my music. A dark fog descended on me. I couldn't concentrate on anything and I shambled about the empty house. We had the two girls, Joan and Norma still working in the shop but I was desperately alone and unhappy. I don't think I ever talked it out with my father. Granma, ninety three years old, walked across the village and 'did' for us. She used to own one of the three pubs in the village – someone said she was preserved in brandy which apparently she consumed a half bottle a day. But she was usually gone when I got back from school.

Church services were torture for me. I sat at the front of the church in the choir and whenever death was mentioned in the service and hymns I just knew that all the people in church were looking at me. I couldn't stand the worry of it and left the choir. I wasn't absolutely sure of where my mum had been buried, but I did go into the cemetery a few times to just stand and think about her.

We had the *Daily Express* newspaper in our house each day. I loved Rupert Bear, but didn't take in much else. I tried to do some of the puzzles but they generally left me flat, then one day there was a headline that some philosophers were going up to the top of a mountain in India to pray and they expected everyone that had recently died to come back again. I went to school that day and in every class I excused myself – diarrhoea – and stood in the quadrangle looking at the sky waiting for her to come back. At the end of the day when we went in the crocodile back to the station I refused and ran down the side of the river Ouze sat on a seat and cried, until two elderly women walking past asked me what was the matter. I couldn't tell them as I was beginning to think how improbable it would be for everyone to return from the dead, and instead ran all the way to the station and just made my regular train.

I gave up real work at school and just concentrated on and played all sports although I still enjoyed geography and did pretty well at it. Now being fourteen I started taking a real interest in girls. Joan in the shop was probably twenty and I made the odd clumsy approach to her but she gently told me to look at the girls at school; but I really wanted some kind of physical contact and went to dancing classes in the village hall.

Olive gave the lessons and it was fine when she told us what to do as we walked through the steps in line, but every time I had to hold her or one of the other girl learners in my arms I got a hardened horn on and gave up as it was embarrassing me. My friend Dick said I shouldn't worry about it, women liked to think they were attractive, but I never felt comfortable with a great protrusion thrusting at the seams of my trousers, and Dick was two year older than me, which was a lifetime in village terms.

CHAPTER 4

I was playing football for the School 1st Team, also played for Rockland as well on Saturdays. I really enjoyed both teams. The school matches would have a crowd of the screaming young who leapt about if we scored, whilst Rockland was much more restrained. Bill Saunders, who was our centre half and very strong, had great backing from his wife who attended all the matches and had a piercing voice. One year Rockland made it to the Norfolk junior cup final which we lost 5-3 but at the end of the game a Norwich City Scout offered me trials for them. And I had played in borrowed boots!!

He said. "Would you like a trial for Norwich City?"

"OK then, when?" I said.

He asked for my address. Excited, I cycled back to Caston with Rex Jolly our coach/manager. He was a marvellous magician and worked at the bakers. You could give him money for your bread, he would ask you to hold out your hand for the change but somehow it missed your hand and ended up in his below. I told him that I was having a trial with Norwich.

He said, "that's great news, when?"

"Oh I don't know, the scout said he would let me know."

A couple of weeks later a letter arrived for me, I was to have my first trial at Poringland, I would be picked up and driven there. A big black car came to pick me up. We also picked up a young man, Jeff from Attleborough. We talked a bit on the way and were both quite nervous as to what was expected of us.

When we arrived I didn't know anyone else and felt a bit lonely but several others were also there for the first time and we were playing with a city youth team. They were so fast. I realised that I was very unfit compared to them, but my love of the game took over. As usual I played at left half but I'm not sure how I did as I was overexcited and didn't show much attacking flair.

After something like a half hour's football the man who had greeted us when we arrived took us all into a hut alongside the ground and said we had done well but he was changing some of us around to see how we fared. We, I guess the trialists, were now mixed with the young city boys and the pace quickened and we played with some stops from the man. And after he whistled for a final stop he said he was happy with us and he would be in touch again soon to arrange our next trial.

Another trial! What excitement, a big black car picked me up and took me to Norwich, Carrow Road, I was somewhat overcome with the size of it all. We went to what was their training ground near Carrow Road. I had a mixed game and several times players were from team to team. I thought I gave a good account of myself, but again I felt slow compared to many of them and I determined to try to get fitter. There were two men in charge of our trial, one said he would be in touch in the next few weeks.

Meanwhile I helped with all the shop things and cooked for dad in the evenings, I started to enjoy that and experimented with bread rolls, which I would fry, melt some cheese in the frying pan and then put a little jam in them. I also made a few soups from anything that was lying around.

My brother had put his age up and joined the Army. But the war was nearly over. My glamorous Auntie Marian, my mother's sister, lived in Norwich and Uncle Aubrey was away in the war, in India. We hadn't seen anything of her since my mum's burial but she did write regularly to my dad and asked him how we all were. My dad replied saying I was to be a trialist at Norwich and could I stay with her.

I would often work on one of the Banham farms, all the cousins and uncles – and there were a few – would work together on all the farms in and around the village. While we worked we saw a few dogfights between our fighters and the Jerries, and had a few bombs drop in and around. We even had some butterfly bombs dropped one weekend.

Alan Breeze was driving a horse and cart loaded with hay when the cartwheel ran over one and blew the cart into pieces, luckily he was unhurt but "thanked his lucky stars" as he said that night in the pub for having a load on. Another farmer we heard in the next village had his horse stand on one and the horse's complete stomach was blown out. The prime move was that my father was loading sheaves onto a wagon on Arthur Banham's farm and he put one up that had a bomb in it. Everything stood still then and the whole village was told to stay in our houses whilst bomb disposal army men arrived and dealt with them. Even so one or two locals had narrow escapes before the realisation set in that they were lethal, one young lady delivering newspapers took a kick at one when on her bicycle but luckily missed it.

The war finished and Granma, pub, was getting too feeble to walk so Aunt Marian came out with Aubrey. He was now a sergeant in the army and was an instant hit with all the locals. He had a bush hat on with his uniform and it had a feather up the side. She persuaded my dad to advertise for a housekeeper, she did the paperwork and put the ad in the *Eastern Daily Press*.

A few days later a really motherly lady arrived and my dad met her and talked, she went away, the next day another lady arrived with a black dog on a lead. Jim, my dog took an instant dislike to this one and spent a while growling.

She stayed and she moved in with all her possessions and took over the house. She cleaned my shoes, she was over attentive and tried hard to win my affections. After a few weeks I heard noises from my dad's bedroom of people in pain. She announced one day they were going to get married and asked what would I wear for the ceremony. I walked over the village to see Dick, my friend. We sat in his garden most of the day and I eventually said, "I can't go to the wedding." So we arranged to go to Thetford for a dance and that I would stay the night with Dick when we got back. I told my dad I wouldn't go to the wedding, which upset them both. I had to go to Thetford and Dick was taking me on his motorbike and I would stay with him overnight. Before I went I thought it would be funny to get the bell from the shop and tie it under their bed.

My stepmother would not speak to me for weeks and any messages were relayed through my dad. I ate alone and spent a great deal of my time in my workshop with Smut and I resolved to leave.

Winter arrived, and the village was snowed in, the vicar had sent round a note for all able bodied people to be on the village green, armed with brushes, spades, pickaxes, buckets and any instrument that would be useful. Virtually the whole village came. It was probably the closest all the inhabitants had been since VE night.

Colonel Hardinge pulled his way onto the 'Pilgrims Stone' in the centre of the green. He announced that the village was cut off by road from both Attleborough and Watton and it was up to all of us to try to dig our way through to Rockland, the next village. The colonel's and the village post office were the only telephones in the village and the wires were down therefore there was no way of knowing if the snowplough from Attleborough was trying to get through.

We all followed the lead of the Colonel and walked past the Red Lion pub, up the main road, past Major Petrie's mansion and puffed our way past Hazells farm to the rise in the road and open country.

Just around the sharp corner we were met with huge snow drifts, the road was completely blocked with snow up to the top of the hedges either side of the road, where it had presumably drifted across the open fields and gradually filled the cavity that had been our road. We all took turns in cutting away at the snow and the women brushed the loose snow up to the hedges, we were digging a trench possibly six feet wide and about nine feet deep, it proved to be hard backbreaking work and we were making slow progress, after a while the younger children started to make snow balls and throw them at each other. A few mums tried to control them but they had tired of working. It developed into a full scale battle and Stoat Breeze ended up on the ground with the local kids stuffing snow into his boots, his neck and any visible orifice.

We worked all day and had made steady progress, eventually arriving at the top of the hill to be met with a group from Rockland who were doing the same thing. The gap we had made was not wide enough for lorries to get through but horses and carts could. There was much celebration and darkness fell as we all trooped back down to the village green where Dick's father offered free drinks from the *Red Lion* to everyone. The grown ups all went for beer and us younger workers had either orange or lemonade. Most of us were quite wet from the snow and our exertions so we welcomed going home to a warm house. It had been a great experience, so many people all working together.

Christmas came and it was the loneliest day of my life, I spent most of the day reading a book or looking at old photos of our family with my beautiful mum smiling in most of them. My dad and Hilda had gone off to the pub for Christmas lunch I had turned down going with them.

I thought of leaving home but if I left where would I go? I would miss Smut my cat, and Jimmy dog was getting really old. I was still at grammar school, my results were so bad apart from geography, but I didn't think it mattered. I didn't really have anyone to discuss leaving with. Could I live with Mike, my friend? I was too young for the forces.

Joan and Norma were still looking after the shop. They were great but my new stepmother took to going in and demanding attention even if they were serving others from the village, and the business started going downhill, so much so one day my dad said he couldn't afford to keep me at Thetford any longer.

She was standing behind him polishing something. He suggested I do some work to help for the rest of that term.

I was still playing a lot of football with the School and Rockland. Saturday mornings I would take my bike to Thetford on the train from Stow Bedon Play in whatever match we had, then cycle back to Rockland, some thirteen miles and play for Rockland in the afternoon. I think I was fit, but I had not heard anything from Norwich City for some time which worried me a bit.

I was very nervous but I told the headmaster that I was leaving school and when he asked why I told him that father had said that he needed me to work as our shop business had failed, but that I thought it was my stepmother influencing him as she didn't like me much. He asked me if I was sure that I wanted to leave as my results were not that good now. I said I had to and told him how much I enjoyed geography and the sport but since my mother died I had had problems with my concentration in most of the classes. The headmaster knew all of this and wished me all good fortune in whatever I did. I thanked him and scuttled off.

CHAPTER 5

I started doing some part time work for my uncle Fred – Blind Fred – as he was known. He had an uncanny ability to walk anywhere on his farm, up to a gate and go straight to the catch holding it.

When he went into the pig yard to feed the pigs they all stood back from the trough until he had emptied the bucket of food. If anyone else did it they would crowd around and knock at the bucket. It was amazing. He could do all the usual things necessary on a farm, use a scythe on grass, trim hedgerows in perfect lines, but, if anyone moved a tumbril, or hand cart, or anything, they had to let him know as he was aware of, and knew exactly, where things were placed.

I quickly tired of being a farm labourer, even though a pretty girl often came to visit Fred and his wife – a cleaner they said. She rode a bike with great style and had a wonderful smile. I thought I knew everyone in our village but as she came from Northacre, I hadn't spent much time there so I paid particular attention to the time of day that she arrived and left. One day we started to talk. I suggested a bike ride to Watton the next Saturday to see a film. We went and sat on the back row, occasionally hand touching then an arm round her shoulders – that was the most thrilling moment!

When we came out I was feeling randy and on the way home I suggested a detour down a lane and we found a grassy bank to lie on, we did a bit of kissing and that turned out to be a fairly desperate encounter. I had for some time kept a 'Johnny' in my possession and after I had got off her hand knitted bra and pants and put on the rubber in what seemed a split second I was away. Panting I tried to joke it away but she was not at all concerned, so there we were searching through her knickers trying to find my Johnny as it was not on me. I looked up and staring at us through a hedge only feet away was this grinning face. I leapt up and shouted and he rushed away. I couldn't get through the hedge to chase him, in truth I wasn't too certain I should as I wasn't feeling sure of myself and my belt and fly buttons were undone. Needless to say the relationship didn't progress from there but I started going to the pictures at Watton on a regular basis sometimes with mates, other times alone. My cousin Betty was an usherette there so I always had company at the end of the films. I saw some wonderful films including the '*Cat and the Canary*' with Bob Hope. Then '*Blue Skies*' with Bing Crosby and Joan Caulfield. I loved that and completely fell for Joan Caulfield she became a regular visitor to my world, we had fun.

I was invited back to Thetford for an old boys football match, I went on the train and was walking towards the school when I called into a greengrocers to buy some apples, as I walked in there she was ... Joan Caulfield, or very close to her, I stared at her and two or three times she asked me what I wanted, I was tongue tied, I eventually asked for my apples and then added.

"Have you seen the film *Blue Skies*?"

She gave me a curious look and said, "No why?"

"Well you are the spitting image of Joan Caulfield and she is my favourite film star."

She coloured a bit and said to a man standing in the doorway behind her "I bet that's his favourite line."

The man came forward and said "No he's right you are a bit like her only prettier." Then she really blushed. I thanked her for the apples and was about to go out when he said "You can pay Brenda for them if you like."

I met up with some of my old football team, but I was in a dream and managed to knock myself out running into a goal post when I attempted a header. As soon as the match finished I said I was leaving.

"Why leave so early," they asked, "we should get some tea and sandwiches."

I hung around with them for a while but couldn't wait to get back to the shop in case she had left. I went back to the greengrocers but she wasn't there, a chap with long hair and a fag hanging out of his mouth was weighing up some potatoes. I looked around.

"Wha do yew want?" he asked,

"Oh nuthin thanks, is Brenda in?"

"So yewr the chap, whats wrong with your face?"

"My face?"

"Yeah you gotta bruise".

I had forgotten my collision.

"Is she here?" I pleaded,

"So you're the toff from the grammar school, She'll be back in a few minutes you can wait outside."

I sat on the window sill and was rapidly running out of confidence, when she suddenly arrived carrying a wrapped parcel and said "Hello did you enjoy your game and what's wrong with your face?"

"Oh I ran into a goal post."

She smiled and then I asked her if I could see her one day next week, she said "Wednesday is my afternoon off, meet me here at one o'clock". It was as easy as that, maybe lines like that are for real. But I really meant it. I was in a dream. I was so nervous as I walked away, I had never been so forward and she had said yes, and she was so beautiful. I went back home and the next day met up with some of my mates on the green for a kick about.

"Not seen much of yew," said Sugar Bailey, "what yew bin doin?"

"I've met a beautiful girl she looks just like Joan Caulfield, the woman in *Blue Skies*."

"Din't see that" says Sugar "but do she bone?"

I was upset at that, and took a kick at a ball that ran along the green.

Bob Childerhouse said "Yew in love then?"

I started to reply then thought, no, just let them carry on, after we had finished I said I was off and when I went to work on Monday told Blind Fred I wanted Wednesday off.

"Why's that?" he asked.

"I've got a date with the most beautiful girl."

"You be careful young Brian, you don't want to get wed yet."

"I'm not thinking of that I'm just pleased to get a date, don't know what I'll do with her as it's the afternoon in Thetford."

"Thetford", he said, "thas a long way away. Not that I've ever bin. Have been to Watton a couple of times and some years ago went to Yarmouth, bought some bloaters I remember."

He was such a lovely man and his Norfolk accent came out at the oddest times.

I started searching the *Eastern Daily Press* 'jobs' page, for attractive things to do. Now I was to be a lover, phew I should get a real job. I was anticipating my date on Wednesday.

The two days passed so quickly then suddenly it was Wednesday morning. I took my bike to Stow Bedon station and as I went through the main entrance the station master said "Hello you're a bit late for school."

"I've finished there." I said.

"Well, have you got a ticket?"

"No."

I had completely forgotten that I would have to buy one as I searched my pockets he said with a grin "You're ok get one coming back."

I got to the station I was early and I hung around the centre of Thetford for a while then the church clock said it was ten to one so I sauntered down the hill towards the shop. She came out in a lovely green dress, my favourite colour, with little short sleeves and a sloping neck line.

"Lets get a snack at the corner café," she said then, "What do you want to do?"

I coloured I knew what I wanted to do… Kiss her, but suggested we walked along the river bank. We each had a sandwich which she insisted on paying for – I wasn't very gallant and let her. Whilst we were eating she leant close to me to look at my bruise and I thought *should I try to kiss her, I'm sure Bing Crosby would have*. But after giving me a long study she said "I'm not really a bit like Joan Caulfield"

"You are, you're definitely prettier."

"I bet you say that to all the girls."

"I don't have any girls. I play football, cricket, billiards in the village hall and fish a bit."

I suddenly realised I was talking naturally to the prettiest girl I had ever seen I got covered in confusion

We started walking along the river bank there was only one other person an old lady with a dog, when we had walked some distance turned the corner we were completely alone and I suggested we lay down in the long grass, she looked around "ok" so we laid alongside each other and I was completely tongue tied. I stared at the river and flicked some sticks into it. I couldn't think of anything to say and she got a bit restless. I draped an arm over her and she didn't move it. I laid down like that for some time on my front in the most excited state.

"I've left the Grammar School now", I eventually said, "but I could come over sometimes if you wanted."

"I've got a boyfriend but he's in the Navel Cadets and is at Dartmouth so I don't see much of him now."

"Oh."

"Why did you leave the grammar school?" she asked

"Oh I think it was because our shop was losing money and they couldn't afford to keep me there."

"Who are they?"

I thought about that question for a minute or so and then told her where I lived, how my mother had died. My father marrying again with someone I didn't get on with. She kept prompting me to carry on and then I told her something that had lived with me for a while. The vicar had come round to our house one day to try to get my stepmother to come to church because as I had left the choir no one else in my family were church goers other than my aunt Alice, dads sister, who lived in Northacre.

When he arrived at our back door he found Hilda burning all our family photos and records, which we had kept in a glass case between the shop and our living room. She had not turned a hair and told him she was not interested in church, when he asked her what she was burning she asked him to leave. He had then told Aunt Alice this and she had told me, I didn't know if she had told my father, but it meant that I only had a couple of photos left of my mother, perhaps Roy had some but I wouldn't know that till he returned from the Army.

She listened and put an arm across me, I felt like crying but I couldn't do that in front of this lovely girl, but I did warm to her as I could not recall ever talking seriously about proper things in my life.

I wanted to change the subject "How old are you and why do work in the greengrocers?" I felt she should be in films or a ladies fashion shop.

"I like it there." she said, "How old do you think I am?"

I didn't know what to say and then said, "About my age I think."

She said, "What's that?"

"Nearly sixteen."

We talked for a while then I said "I have to go home soon as I have to cook my dad's meal."

We got up a bit crumpled. I had to put my hand in my pocket to arrange my trousers and we walked back mainly in silence up the bridge.

"Can I see you again, can I write to you?"

"Yes and yes but it would be best to the greengrocers."

She gave me the address and I went off. I didn't look back because I had seen John Wayne in a film walk away from a girlfriend. But I longed to see if she was waving.

On the train I thought of all the things I could have said. I glowed with excitement – *I had been on a date with a beautiful girl.* I had talked closely with her, it meant a lot to me and I resolved to see much more of her. But I hadn't tried to kiss her, *would she have let me?* I wondered. I would write to her I thought. I spent a lot of time writing, then crumpling the paper.

Great news, a letter came from Norwich City, *Could I get to Carrow Road the following week, on Monday morning.* I told my dad that I would take my bike and the few clothes that I possessed and go to Aunt Marians on Sunday.

I put everything I wanted in my carrier which I had made for my bicycle and I wanted Joan to look after Smut as I obviously couldn't take her to Norwich. I wrote to Brenda and said I was going to Norwich City for trials so it might be some time before I could come to Thetford again, but I really wanted to see her again. I cycled to Norwich to my Aunt Marians and told her I was going on an apprenticeship scheme to the football club. My uncle Aubrey was very impressed and kept congratulating me, "but I'm only on trial" I insisted.

"I'm sure you will make it" he said.

I settled in with them, came Monday morning I woke early, then cycled to Carrow Road feeling very nervous, I met another young man, Keith, from Lincolnshire. He had been at the Poringland trial.

The kindly man that we had met there asked me if I wanted digs and I told him I was staying with my aunt in Upper Hellesdon. He said, "there are five of you new to us and we will start here with some basic training, my main concern is to see your fitness level, then we go for a five a side game at our training ground".

We started something he called circuit training! I had I thought I was fit but I soon realised that I was far from it, particularly when we had to run up and down the terracing.

They took about fifteen of us to another pitch with a very small clubhouse. I started playing – initially at left half, then the coach, who had been joined by another man, mixed us up as some of the young men were already in the city A team. I was enjoying playing and felt I was improving when suddenly *BANG!* I was badly kicked in the knee – my left cartilage – and it swelled to an enormous lump. The coach arranged a car to take me to the Norfolk and Norwich Hospital. The only thing I could think about was my bike and I said to the coach "I've got my bike here can you keep it safe."

My leg was operated on which was incredibly painful and the plaster was on for nearly three weeks. My aunt and uncle came in two or three times a week to bring books and grapes, she also got me to do some crocheting work on a cushion cover. When they took the plaster off my leg was very white and feeble. I went back Marian and Aubrey and she fussed over me. When I went to Carrow Road, still limping and not very content, I was told after some discussion that I would not make the grade. Just like that I was finished with the only thing I really wanted to do and so young.

CHAPTER 6

I didn't have any idea of what to do, I thought of staying with Aunt Marion in Norwich, but then went back to Caston. I immediately realised I couldn't live there with my stepmother. It was at the start of the sugar beet time, my brother had come home from the army and got a job lorry driving, I guess that his driving of tanks in the army got him the job.

I wrote to the other city boy I had started with and got to know quite well, Keith. He told me he had heard that Gainsborough Trinity were looking for part time pros. *Where's Gainsborough?* I thought that films were made there, so that excited me a bit. I eventually got my brother to take me and my bike on a lorry load of sugar-beet to the station at Thetford. It was still quite early in the morning and he was going on to the refinery at Bury St Edmunds. He said on the way he had met a lovely girl who lived near Norwich and he was going to live with her and probably get married as he felt he wasn't welcome with Hilda.

When he dropped me near the station I thought this is an ideal opportunity to see Brenda, who had taken a back seat in my thoughts during the football time. I cycled down to the greengrocers shop and the old nervous excitement came back, maybe I could stay in Thetford and get some work and really see her every day. I leant the bike against the sill and went in, there was yet another man behind the counter that I had not seen before.

"Is Brenda in?" I asked

"No she's on holiday this week. I believe she has gone to Devon or Cornwall, Dartmouth I think."

"Oh when will she be back?"

"Next Monday."

It was only Tuesday so I thanked him and told him to tell her I had called in. "Brian is my name."

With my few belongings I caught a train to Lincoln and then Gainsborough. Eventually I got there, found the Gainsborough Trinity football club, told them I had been injured at Norwich, asked for a trail, and was offered one later in the week, an evening with the rest of the team and other trialists.

"Have you any idea where I could find lodgings here?" I asked the man in their office.

"Yes we have one or two places where some of our team live."

He gave me three addresses. I found digs with a school teacher and his wife, he was a local hero in the snooker hall, and was one of the top players in Lincolnshire. The family made me welcome but it was a polite relationship with the three of them. They had a particularly lovely daughter who was going out with a nice young man that worked in Rose Brothers – a wrapping machinery firm. He suggested I could try them for work as most of the Gainsborough Trinity team were part time anyway even if I did make the grade there.

I played in a trial match where I was asked to play inside left. I had done very little training or running since my operation and when I told the manager this, he said, "Ok we will just see how your reactions are today then I suggest a fitness programme and we can have another trial."

I played for about half an hour and he said "That's enough, get yourself fit."

I went cap in hand to Rose Brothers to see if I could get an apprenticeship as an engineer. I had the name of the MD and asked if I could see him. The lady at reception asked me who I was and why I wanted to see the MD. I was a bit embarrassed but said I was looking for an apprenticeship with the company as I was very keen to become an engineer. She pointed me in the direction of a youngish man that was dressed in blue overalls, when I asked him if he was the MD he laughed and said, "No, I'm the general foremen of the fitting shop and I usually interview anyone that rolls up off the street."

"Do you get many people doing that" I asked.

"No, we do have an apprenticeship scheme which is advertised in local papers but, very few people just roll up".

I told him of my landlady's daughter's boyfriend who had suggested I approach the company, when I said who I lived with he said "Yes we will give you a trail".

My head spun, a trial, this was like a football club. Is all of life going to start with a trial?

"How does the trial work?" I asked

"Well you will work for a few days with the supervisor in the shop, he will see that you are taught the correct way to handle all the tools and if you are ok you can also go to the technical college one day a week to learn the technical aspects of fitting and engineering."

Coo did I want to go back to school, the memories were not that attractive, but I said "Fine thank you, what shall I do now?"

I was introduced to the supervisor, another blue clad man who seemed friendly enough.

"You can start next week."

I spent the rest of the week trying to get myself fit and went to the cinema twice. Then I started working. Rose Brothers manufactured all kinds of wrapping machinery. I spent a few days desperately trying to impress my supervisor of my eagerness to learn. I got on pretty well with most of the people in the fitting shop and Yes, they would employ me as an apprentice. Yes, I could have one day a week at the Tech college.

Rose Brothers also had a big sports ground so I would do some running, press ups, kicking footballs with some other apprentices and workers from the company each evening, and I went back to The Trinity as they were called and said I was ready for another trial. The manager told me at the end that I was a long way from fitness and suggested I rectify that if I wanted to get on there. I took that as a no.

I started eyeing up the daughter at my lodgings and one night a crowd of us went to a dance in Worksop and on the bus coming back I sat with her and asked her if I could be first reserve while her fella was away doing his national service. When we got back to the house her parents were in bed and we dallied a little on the carpet in front of the last few embers in the fire. I was very new to the art of lovemaking and asked her how I could learn to live.

Somehow the family got to know I fancied their daughter and they not very politely told me to leave. I had made friends with one of the other apprentices named Paul Waterland and I moved in with him. He was lodging with a lovely family overlooking the football ground and I still held aspirations of making a career with The Trinity. It was easy to get in and use their facilities and I managed to train on some evenings but I eventually dropped the idea of professional football. Because I was sharing the lodgings with Paul we became very good friends. Paul was very keen on gambling on the horses, in a small way, and then he became a runner for a bookie in the town. I also helped and we would collect bets from several of the workers in Rose Bros., and either he or I would cycle to deliver them to the bookie, we managed to raise a few pounds illegally from this.

My landlady was very proud of her two boys and showered love on us. Her husband had the most terrifying cough I had heard and one day he told us that during the 1914 war he had been badly injured and thrown on a cart as dead; the cart was being pulled away when someone noticed a faint movement in one of his legs, they dragged him off the cart and he was eventually nursed back to health. The soldier that had noticed him survived and had kept in touch and they were firm friends.

I made two other very good friends, Alfie Raynsworth and Cedric 'Ceddy' Brown. Ceddy had a lovely sister that went under the nickname of United Nations, she was popular with everyone, I had acquired 'Lady Chatterleys Lover' and on one very sunny weekend she and I read this on the banks of the river Trent that went through Gainsborough. We had found an isolated place in some bushes. And I enjoyed the book and in a limited way Ceddy's sister. It had quite a history, the river. Apparently twice a year it would virtually drain and then where it carried out into the Humber, near Hull a great flood would occur.

It was named 'A bora' and a tidal wave rushed down the river, sometimes twelve or more feet high. To watch it race through Gainsborough was very exciting and there was a young gipsy man that used to dive into it off the main bridge. He was eventually stopped by the constabulary as it was too dangerous and could inspire others to do the same.

Alfie was a butcher and Ceddy an apprentice architect at Rose Brothers, we used to cycle to various places and one weekend taking our little tents we had gone to Mablethorpe, a small village on the coast. The sands there were superb, flat and vast; horses were trained there, but very little else seemed to happen. At a music arcade, over a juke box, I met a very pretty girl from Sheffield that was with her family on holiday. We hit it off and when it was time for us to cycle back she then invited me to her house in Parsons Cross, north side of Sheffield. The next weekend I went by bus and eventually found her place. Her dad was a coal merchant and she had ten other brothers and sisters in a three bedroom house.

Sheffield Wednesday were at home that Saturday so six of us went in his coal lorry and watched the great Derek Dooley hit a hat-trick. I slept on the settee and the first morning I woke up to find a little bare bottom about a foot above my face and a little fella saying "wake up Johnny" That was my name then!! When I started playing football for the Rose Bros works team they already had a Brian in the team and as it was common practice during a match to call out the teams names if you could help out or demand a pass.

The Sunday social scene in Sheffield for everyone seemed to be waiting for the pub to open and drink as much as you could before closing time. Several of us had got into her father's lorry to drive back to their house and he hit a telegraph pole. It was leaning to about 45 degrees so he turns the lorry round and run into it from the other side more or less straightening it. Mid-afternoon I said I had to get back and Doreen, my so called girlfriend walked me to the bus and I left ... Never to return ... Many years later I bumped into her in the Tower Ballroom in Blackpool, she was married and owned a small hotel there.

My apprenticeship meant studying at the local tech college, but on my first day there the lecturer told me I would do better on a market stall. This didn't worry me too much as I hated the clocking in and the dismal level of enjoyment in the firm, but I did manage to get a set of indentures to show that I had served a full apprenticeship as an engineering fitter. I had a fling with the MD's daughter and she somehow provided me with the articulated forms!! The firms football team gave me some encouragement but I quickly tired of Gainsborough (They didn't make films there) and decided that I wanted to fly so tried to take up a career in the air force and went to RAF Cranwell and during various tests I was told I was colour blind. I didn't believe the tests but was assured that I could not fly, so decided to do my National Service in the RAF.

CHAPTER 7

My initial training involved lots of square bashing at Bridgenorth. I didn't like the DI's, drilling instructors, but we were meant to dislike them. They all had very short haircuts and were a belligerent lot whose sole aim seemed to be to make us feel totally useless.

I quickly worked out how to get in the middle rank for marching, by making sure I was second, fifth, eighth, or eleventh in line, then as we straightened out I would be middle rank, that way you were shielded and when we started marching by some deft footwork you could throw the whole system to much cursing and some laughter from the following men.

This was fine but on my actual passing out parade final rehearsal, I couldn't get in the middle and ended up on the front rank. Having spent so much time trying to march out of step I found it difficult to do so and as we marched along the parade ground I was suddenly confronted by the officer in charge screaming at me for being useless and he then banned me from the final parade. In one respect that didn't worry me as I didn't have any relatives coming, so I sat in the barracks window and watched, heaving a sigh of relief as I really didn't enjoy anything smacking of regimentation.

Social life there was very limited, we had had very little money so big spends were out. Bridgenorth wasn't the centre of social activity but I did have one experience, I had gone to a dance and got along well with a girl and somehow, can't think why, I found myself on a very late bus going to Glazeley with her, about three miles from Bridgenorth. On getting to her house I managed a quick feel and a promise of more next Saturday.

I then had to walk back though a very lonely countryside, on nearing Bridgenorth the road was through a forest with very high banks and walking along in pitch black conditions I suddenly saw a white skull roll down the bank about 20 yards ahead of me. I was petrified and looked around for a stick as I was sure someone was there and I would be attacked. Nothing, I just stood and gazed at the skull, I then found a dead branch that was lying on the side of the road and plucking up courage started to slide past the skull, as I got nearer it took on a different appearance and I then poked it with my stick and it disintegrated. It was the root of a tree.

I made it to the camp and was challenged by the sentry on duty and questioned as to who I was even though I was in my scratchy uniform. When I was able to tell him which group I was with he reluctantly let me in but said, "You're very late, hope you got your end away".

I smiled knowingly and trotted off. I had no ties, so volunteered to go abroad, but was posted to Stafford. Two years in bloody Stafford.

I joined in all the sports, soccer, cricket, started throwing the hammer and putting the shot, played tennis for the camp with a lovely Squadron Officer lady as my partner and wore dreadful shirts with leaping lions on my chest!! I qualified for the finals at Uxbridge in the hammer and shot putting. I believe I was RAF champion for the hammer for about two minutes until Flying Officer, Mark Pharoah stepped up and swung it out of sight, he later threw for England. When I returned to Stafford I was made a corporal (I guess for my efforts) was put in charge of the sports store and also had my own billet with a rowdy group of young men.

My days were pretty easy, so I also ran the library on some evenings and took some pleasure in fining my mates if they were late returning their books.

As a corporal I earned a bit more money and I bought a motorbike, a fish tail Velocett, very second hand. This gave me freedom to get out at the weekends and on one Saturday night I went to Trentham Gardens dance night, met up with a lovely girl from Stone, a large village quite near Stafford. Her parents had some shops there, she had a small convertible car and I became a welcome visitor and met up with a wide circle of her friends. One night I had invited her to a dance on the camp in the winter, she had been brought there by her sister and I was to take her home on the motorbike, during the dance it had turned frosty, not that I realised this, but on the way back I had come up a slight incline and when we got over the top I hit some ice and the bike slipped away from me and we were both sliding down the hill. I made the mistake of going to the bike first which was lying on its side wheels still spinning. She hadn't been hurt just shocked. It took some time to repair my relationship with her and she was banned from ever riding it again by her father.

In some respects life for me started in the RAF. I was exposed to a wide range of young men from all walks of life. I made two particular friends, a Dave Barton, nicknamed Dick of course, and Keith Sutherland, who was a lovely guy from the Lake District. We had some scrapes and great times. Dick had been in the merchant navy and could swear in Hindustan, which he did at length when he got drunk. He was also a dab hand at throwing the axe, which we had for chopping the wood in our billet in the winter. Keith would stand by the back door and Dick would throw the axe at him, usually missing him, Keith did keep his eyes shut … Great cabaret ..

We, the three of us, raided a garden one night and collected a great bunch of rhubarb. Dick said he knew how to make rhubarb wine. We scrounged bottles from the NAAFI and one of the Stafford pubs and brewed this at night in an unused billet. We had some 25 bottles stored above our bunks. On a particularly hot day Flight Lt Leonard decided to do an inspection and in the middle of it one of the bottles exploded and rained down wine onto Taffy's bed.

I think the Lieutenant had got wind of our brewing and wanted to check. I was asked to remove all of it or supervise it being poured into the ground at the back of the billet. At the same time my billet and twenty men were relocated into a new billet that was just completed. Taffy managed to purloin two bottles and take to his new surroundings. A few nights later several of us came back to the camp to find Taffy absolutely plastered and being very ill. He was completely stiff, couldn't move a muscle, he stayed like that for several hours but eventually came round and was fine, other than dreadful farts that suffocated the whole room..

One night I had gone into the RAFA club in Stafford in civvies, with some of my mates and after two pints of 'Mr Fisher' a mixture of cider and Guinness, I was feeling on top of the world. Ian Mitchell and I decided to go to the town hall as we heard that there was a fancy dress arts ball on. We were never challenged and walked in, found our way to a bar that had drinks lined up on the counter but no one in charge, Ian helped himself to a bottle of gin I took a bottle of brandy and we went into a corner and proceeded to swig most of it. I woke up next morning in jail, RAF jail, with Ian. We were marched down to the cookhouse, for breakfast, still in our civvies and we were still very drunk marching out of step and singing the Sheik of Araby, much to the disgust of the sergeant that was marching us. In the cookhouse we threw a few fried eggs around and were then marched back to the jail.

After a while I was made to stand in front of Flight Lt Leonard who was on duty for the weekend, he fined both Ian and me five shillings and said how disappointed he was in us. "But Sir I don't remember what I did."

"Corporal Banham, you were arrested standing on the bar reciting some poems much to the amusement of some of the art students but one of the organisers reported you to the Red caps, that's why you are in front of me. Don't let it happen again."

I staggered out to be met by Dick Barton, "Come on we're going to my wedding. You're my best man and we have to get to York by 2 o'clock."

We caught a train and at every stop he jumped out and bought a Lucozade which I drank and gradually came round. I went through the wedding in a haze, managed to produce the ring he had given me at the correct time and we went off in convoy to the reception. One glass of champagne and I was over the top. I have no idea what I said, much of it about Dick and his antics but apparently Dick's mother loved it, his dad, the council's chief engineer wasn't impressed.

I decided to take a course in photography, and bought a Voigtlander camera which became my constant companion. Just before my great demob day and departing from the air force I went to London to Pimlico to see a famous photographer to, I hoped, get work.

"Can I see your portfolio?" his secretary receptionist asked.

"I don't have one of those." I replied.

"He won't see anyone without some indication of their work."

So I took a train back again.

Eventually I was demobbed and, in my new demob suit, I went to my aunt's in Norwich. My thoughts turned to a job as I only had thirty five pounds to my name.

I went to Great Yarmouth and talked to some of the 'photographers' on the front, Happy snaps, could I work with them? I had seen Billy Butlin at a reception in Filey and got photographed with him some years before, so I wrote to Butlins asking for a job as a photographer. A letter came back almost immediately offering me work on developing and printing holiday pictures and, if suitable, some photographic input for the *News Chronicle* at Skegness, which ran a daily sheet of pictures from the Butlins camps. I acquired a Rollieflex camera on the never-never, that did the trick.

CHAPTER 8

I went to Skegness and lived in a chalet with another photographer, Jim Hodgkinson, who was also a movie maker out of season. I had a great time – anyone who was 'staff' was a hit with the ladies. I also met a great crowd of other staff, the redcoats were all budding comedians or actors. One I particularly got on well with was a young Irishman named Dave Allen with a short first finger. He was to go on and make a name for himself as one of our leading comedians.

The social life at Butlins was very limited for all of the 'staff' but on Friday nights there was always a party when we would try to catch up in one night with the campers' week. Saturday was changeover day so we could amuse ourselves until late afternoon when the various campers activities started. One of our regular events if it was warm and sunny, would be to have a donkey derby on the 'Butlins beach' One of the chefs was a bookie in the off season, he would run a book and we would have six races, all of us taking turns to ride the donkeys and it was chaos but great fun. Sometimes the donkeys would race, other times they would just dig in their hoofs and refuse any temptations.

It was over three months of activity and friendship which I thoroughly enjoyed and was sad to finish but several of us promised to keep in touch. Many of the staff went back to London as the season finished, I decided to go to Blackpool. Their season was much longer because of the illuminations. It was also somewhere that I had visited whilst in the RAF, and slept in a bus shelter. The illuminations had already started when I arrived. I scoured the front for any photography work and came across a Brian Clark and he took me on. He had a display stall on the seafront taking happy snaps. The crowds at Blackpool were four or five deep along the front and I would blag them in, either to have their faces through lovely bodies or sitting on the back of a lion and other 'amusing' templates. We also 'snapped' them walking past and tried to get them to stop and invest in their photos. When they had we would 'take' another one 'just to be sure'. I enjoyed the exposure and made quite a good living for a couple of months as I had a commission on the number of pictures I sold.

I was living with a Mr and Mrs Taylor who ran a boarding house in Buchanan Street. She was very set in her cooking and had a regular pattern of meals. Every morning I was offered fried eggs, bacon, sausage and fried bread. After several days of the same diet I politely enquired if I could have a variety some days.

"What would you like?" she said.

"Perhaps poached eggs on toast."

"I don't have a poacher."

"Well you can put them in water with a little vinegar and they will poach."

For the next week I was given poached eggs. One night I was having a bath and went to sleep in it with the water still running until I was woken up with shouts from Mr Taylor outside as it was leaking into the kitchen below.

"Keep your hair on," I shouted back and turned the taps off, he was bald and didn't take kindly to my observation and after some words I left and moved in with Nancy, a lovely teacher who had just got back from Borneo where she had been teaching Shell Oil people's children.

I had met her at the Tower ballroom one Saturday night. She tried to teach me to play golf and other things.

The season had finished and I needed money to keep up the fun. I thought of deep sea fishing. I had met a whaler one night at the Tower Ballroom and he had boasted of how much money he made. He worked out of Fleetwood, just up the road from Blackpool!! I found myself on a bus going to Fleetwood. I can't remember my exact feelings on the journey. I can remember very clearly the dirty rusty weather-beaten boats tied up at the quayside. Brawny, mainly bearded men, were doing their 'things' on board.

Net repairing I thought. I hadn't really thought out my approach. I don't think I really understood why I was there. Maybe the sea and getting away was attractive. I studied the boats with apprehension. What was I a non-swimmer doing, about to sign on as a deep sea fisherman?

I walked along the quay and I called down to one bearded man and asked him where to go to get a job on a fishing boat. He looked up from his work and studied me for what seemed an age, then directed me in fine clear Scots to forget it. I suppose I must have had some positiveness as I asked again where I should go. He pointed further along the quayside and said the green office. I went along to the green door in what looked like a railway carriage with a flat roof and was met with very hot air as I entered. There was a huge man with only one arm sitting at the far end of the room drinking tea from an enormous mug, he looked up and, "What do yee want"? Scottish again.

"I want to sign on for deep sea fishing I believe you have whalers here."

"Do you have any idea what it's like boy, deep sea fishing?"

"Well no."

"Freezing cold, slipping, sliding on slime, stinking of fish. Do you know what happens on these trips boy, have you seen the inside of a whaler?"

He fired a string of questions and reduced me to silence. As I stood there gazing at him he suddenly softened and said in a totally different voice. "Your first trip pays for your gear, as a greenhorn you will get all the filthy jobs, if you're in the slightest way sensitive you will get bits of fish in your bed, your boots, your pockets, maybe your underpants, and you won't sleep, every trip lasts a minimum of eight days. My advice is to forget it. You wouldn't last a day. But, thank you."

I scuttled out of the office.

I had my camera I took several photos of the boats on the quay, the bearded man was not on his boat when I walked past. It was cold and damp, why had I ventured out to this dump? I caught the next bus back to Blackpool and totally forgot the experience until many years later when my oldest daughter begged me to tell her a true story before she went to sleep – she was tired of 'Cecil Sock.'

I told Nancy that they had no jobs at present. She said "I bet you're glad". I searched the local newspapers job column and found an advert offering 7/6 pence an hour. I went to the named address, a dingy back street, climbed some stairs and was met by a little man in a mac.

"Can you speak English?" he asked

"Yes." I replied,

"You've got the job."

"But, wait a minute, what is it?"

"Betterware Brushes, you will make a success," he said.

I believed him and he whisked me off to Preston to a sales meeting. There were some thirty fellas in a Nissan hut with church pews in lines on both sides of the hall. We sat and wait and then striding down the centre was this big shiny guy with an American accent, who said, "Stand up please. You are all potential managers, you are all going to make a lot of money."

He then handed out some sheets of paper to us all and on it was a poem. It wasn't a poem it was a song. He started to conduct and we sung to the tune of Onward Christian soldiers, the Betterware hymn.

Onward Betterware salesmen

Marching door to door,
With your bag of brushes carrying before,
You will be successful
You will make the sales
You will earn more money etc etc...

He gave us a lecture on techniques for selling door to door. Always be prepared, know your products, have your bag open when they open the door.

Did I make money? Well I did have a lot of fun with some housewives. I perfected a way of getting the bag open and inside the door. I also acquired a bunch of tiny needle threaders which I thought I could give as a present. I also had a little card printed which boldly stated ...*Your Betterware man will call tomorrow and give you a present*... I would stuff these cards in all the doors in a couple of streets each day and follow them up the next day. The next step was to stand at the door with my case firmly closed and when the lady of the house slightly opened the door with a "not today thanks", I would say that's fine but here is your present anyway. And as I went to leave, most of them would say, "Well what have you got in the bag?"

One doctors wife took me in most mornings and we would 'play' on the carpet and she would always buy a baby hair brush, the cheapest line in my bag. One day I called as usual to start my day and was told goodbye. Apparently her husband had found the brushes and complained they didn't even have a baby.

I carried on for some time with Betterware, living with Nancy, trying to play golf at St Annes until the wanderlust took over and I returned to London on an overnight sleeper bus to save money. We had agreed that Nancy would come to visit me once I had established myself and found a flat or a room. I slept some of the way but also gave thought to what I was doing. I didn't know if I had the depth of feeling to really care about anyone, losing my mother so early and having to fend for myself had deeply affected me and had created in me such a void that I couldn't see it being filled. I resolved that I would be honest with Nancy and write to tell her that she should forget me.

CHAPTER 9

I stayed at the RAFFA club near Marble Arch and started looking around for photography jobs. I met up with Jim Hodgkinson, the Butlins movie maker for lunch, and in a café the second day I met up with a man who was in charge of all the services at Olympia. He wanted someone to look after all the exhibitors services, water, lights, gas, electrics etc. for the Ideal Homes Exhibition.

"Was I used to handling people."

"Yes I was."

"OK you'll do."

Olympia. What a place. I had to make sure all the exhibitors got their services in order. Yes there was demand for electricity, gas, water, several of them had cooking facilities, including Fanny Craddock and Johnny. Boy, was she a handful. She caused more aggravation than all the other exhibitors put together – everything had to be perfect.

I enjoyed the challenge and all the workers used to congregate in an upstairs room for their lunch break with their own catering. I started a 'champion' darts competition knockout, during the break. Everyone put in five shillings to enter and I made sure they were all photographed during the event which lasted two weeks and I also designed a cardboard cup which was presented to the winner. I kept the five bob towards my expenses of film and photos.

When that finished I started looking for a flat, I had a bit of money and wandering down Edgeware road I came across a newspaper shop with some ads. One I particularly liked, offering a room in Maida Vale with a professional family.

I telephoned and a lilting Irish voice answered. "Yes?", she gave me the address and I found my way to Elgin Avenue. The door was opened by a startlingly beautiful Irish lady with reddish hair and the most beguiling smile. "Come in". We talked, she was wonderful. I quickly settled that I would be her very first lodger. I would have my own room but share everything else. She had two daughters and a powerful banker husband.

"What did I do?"

"I was a photographer."

I went back to the RAFFA club, collected my few things and set off for my new home.

I decided to become a 'child photographer' and started going door to door canvassing, trying to sell the idea. Again I had great success with the mums. I did photograph a few babies but it was a hard slog and one night in the local pub I met an engineer who worked at Heinz Baked Beans in Harlesden. He said they were looking for a night shift maintenance man. I had my indentures somewhere and on finding them went to Heinz and got the job. It consisted of me going round all the machines after the last shift had finished, oiling them when necessary and then sleeping in the rafters where I had made a bed, until the early morning cleaners arrived. And they paid me. After about six weeks I decided I had had enough of 57 varieties and told them I was leaving. Their manager really worked hard at keeping me on but I was seeing quite a lot of my landlady during the days, when I was meant to be sleeping at home and we became very friendly. I didn't want work to get in the way.

In the next flat to us was a charming Canadian, Clair Cole. He was a chemist and a lover of life. I met him one Saturday as I was about to go out to the tennis courts behind our apartment. I was going to play with my landlady. Clair said "Hey I'm one of Canada's leading tennis players can I join you?"

"Sure."

He arrived ten minutes later with a racket that had about ten strings in it and he was hopeless, but we became good friends and he had a company that produced a variety of products, two of which were Car Pack and Mend-a-pipe. He wanted a demonstrator for his products at exhibitions around the country and also the next Ideal Home Exhibition in Olympia, would I be interested?

I also got a job with the *Little Swedish Club* as their photographer. They had a weekly show and I photographed a few performing celebrities including Eartha Kitt. Jim Hodgkinson, my old Butlins friend, was working at a photographic shop just off Baker Street and he did my developing and printing.

It was after I had produced a life size photo of Eartha Kitt that was going to be stood outside the entrance to the club, that I was propositioned. I brought it from Maida Vale to Soho in a taxi – I couldn't fit her in and had to stick her legs out of the window. The manager asked me up to his office at the top of the building, offered me my pay and also offered me the use of his tongue. He said, "I can do wonderful things with my tongue."

I got up and said, "Is this the last job I do for you, is there a condition?"

"No" he said, "forget I spoke."

I said, "I am very happy with my girlfriend, I have no desire to have any involvement with men OK?"

My landlady, the lovely Mandy had expressed an interest in buying an upright piano and luckily I had a friend in Notting Hill who had one for sale, so we went off together one evening to look at it and she decided to buy it. We had gone by the tube and to celebrate we went into a pub in Notting Hill. After a couple of gin and tonics we decided to take a taxi back home. We had left the rather precise banker husband at home looking after the girls. In the taxi she told me that her husband hadn't any real interest in her, which was why she worked one night a week in the *Renaissance* club in South Kensington, to keep herself sane she said. I had wondered about that occupation of hers as one of her best Irish friends was at the time Maid Marion in *Robin of Sherwood Forest* and I guessed she was mixing with the film crowd there.

Somehow in the taxi our hands held and, she became my tutor and willing partner.

After a fairly tumultuous time her husband discovered this and I was banished from the apartment but only moved a short distance to Edgware road where Clair had previously moved, as he had fallen out with his wife. Clair and I became very close and also in the house were three Indian fellas, one was a pilot with Air India, one the manager of Air India at Heathrow and the third was 'Prince' Jonny Mehra, a lovely character who set off each day with a very large suitcase, stuffed I believe with a variety of Indian nick nacks that everyone wanted!!

Very often the wonderful smell of curry permeated the top floor of the house and I said how marvellous it seemed. They promised me a meal in one of the best Indian restaurants in London, we went to the *Star of India* in Bayswater and I couldn't believe how wonderful food could be. I sweated profusely as I tucked into the various dishes they had ordered, which amused them. We had parties in the house as there were six small flats there and Jonny was the life and soul of them all. I continued seeing Mandy whenever possible, but the urgency began to diminish and I was also working with my camera at the *Little Swedish Club*.

One of the acts, a Mike Lee, and I became friendly and during one of our drinking sessions he told me of a part time job that he did with the AA, in their break-down services team. They had four teams of twelve, all men in each, writers, actors, layabouts, all did shift work answering break-down calls. I went to their offices, met a chap called Sid and we got on well, I told him a bit about myself and he was pleased to offer me a job. We got paid in advance, the shifts were 8am to 5pm. 5pm to 10.30 and 10.30 until 8am next morning. Then two days off. It was a riot, we could also get stand-ins, exchanges from other shifts if we had to have a few days off for other activities.

The AA then were in Fanum House, Leicester Square, the very heart of London. It was a key and lamp set up, twelve stations and we would click into a flashing light and sort out the drivers in trouble. We also, late at night, used to cross-refer lorry drivers with gents or ladies and listen to the confusion. And a card school was the norm after midnight, although we did have camp beds supplied to grab a few hours sleep. I met one man who was to have a lot of influence on my life and become a great friend. I also realised I could fit in the demonstration job for Clair around the AA hours. I bought a scooter which I used around London, and parked it in front of the AA building when I was there.

I then started working for Clair at the Ideal Homes Exhibition, we shared a stand with a Peter Mitchell who was demonstrating, selling a portable combined vice and wood holder. He was a part time school teacher of English and a writer, or so he claimed. One embarrassing evening, we had gone with his wife to see *The Mousetrap* and we were on the front row of the circle, when the play finished and applause was all round us she leapt to her feet and suddenly started shouting that it was a pale shadow of her husband's play '*Death in Deep Freeze*' she was ushered out by two young men that had been selling ice cream at the interval. Apparently Peter had written two plays and this one had been performed at a small theatre in Richmond and had not been successful.

Selling Mend a Pipe and Car Pack was a hoot. I had a bent piece of metal with a dent in it that Claire had fashioned and I had to smear the Car Pack in this dent and fill it, smoothing it off and telling my audience that it would solidify. The Mend a Pipe gave me much pleasure as it was a bit like a good porridge mixture of a white compound.

I would lay out a strip of linen that was used as a bandage if one had cut themselves, spread the mixture along it, wrap it around the pipe and it would solidify, or so Claire insisted.

One early evening I had quite a crowd round me and as I demonstrated a voice from the back said "It doesn't work."

I called him forward, "What do mean it doesn't work, did you do it as I demonstrated?"

"Yes." he said.

"Show me."

He laid out a bit of linen, spread some mixture on it and then wrapped it round the pipe.

"Ah", I said. "I see the problem, you wrapped it from the left over, you should do it the other way round."

"Oh" he said, "then I better have another pack."

I was successful and at one stage ran out of product and Clair had to drive to their factory near Birmingham to keep me going.

Meanwhile Peter Mitchell said that where he lived, at the back of Ladbroke Grove the ground floor flat in his house was to let, it had two bedrooms and a kitchen and would I like it. I was keen to get my own flat and I had made a few pounds so after checking it arranged to take it on with the landlord. I offered the second bedroom to Paul Barnes, a trumpeter I had met at Butlins though at that time he was working for the Publishers Collins, with Peter's wife. I spent a Christmas day with Peter, his wife and a good friend of theirs that was a courier for holidays in Russia. After a good meal and a fair bit of wine we decided to play Monopoly and after some time I started to work with the courier against Peter and Doreen his wife, so much so that Peter got extremely angry and disappeared, he came back with a pistol and said he would shoot us if we carried on ganging up on him. It all ended in good spirits but it made for an interesting day.

CHAPTER 10

I was still interested in football and was playing football with a team in Golders Green. Someone I had met at Butlins had introduced me to them and during one training session I broke my achilles tendon. I managed to ride my scooter to the New End Hospital at Hampstead, fell off it and crawled into the reception. I was immediately put into a bed and operated on the next morning. The surgeon commented on the break and made a double level of cord binding to ensure it wouldn't happen again.

The ward was round and there was a mixture of patients. In the next bed to me was a famous hairdresser named Alvin from Golders Green and every visiting hour he was swamped with his pretty staff and family. On the other side I had the most interesting man, Paul Polak, who was an astrologer. His huge black beard lay out on the blanket and he would look at a nurse and tell her her birthday. I found this fascinating, what a way to get the birds!!

What could I do? I would like to get into his circle. He told me I could study Chiromancy, reading palms. He had the original book, I started to read and became hooked.

I also managed to telephone Mandy one day and told her what had happened, she said life was impossible for her at the moment and she couldn't possibly come to see me as she knew she was being followed whenever she left the house and her husband had threatened her on occasions with pushing her out of the flat and not having access to the children, so with some tears she said she could not see me.

We had an old boy of sixty-odd in the ward, Pop Gale, and he took a special interest in me. We played crib together, he was very deaf and tended to speak in a very loud voice. I organised a knock out cribbage competition between all those that played the game. And Pop eventually won it. We got him onto a trolley and one of the walking wounded pushed him round the ward as we all clapped him, he was thrilled. He also used to wake up with a stiffy each morning and he would call over to me, "Mr Banham, its there again," pushing his stiff arm up into the air.

One of my mates, Graham from the AA, came in to see me and brought his sister. She lived in Belsize Square, not far from the hospital and we got on well, so well she started to come in two or three times a week, bringing with her scotch and sympathy. (She lived with six other girls in a large house and it was called, The Nunnery. It became a popular house and I became a welcome guest, it also meant I could supply several girls for the many parties that happened around the Hampstead area, as they were all unattached) One night we were all woken up with one of the patients yelling loudly and trying to jump out of a window, His outline was against the window with his both arms aloft, luckily the duty nurse that night was a man who grabbed him and after some persuasion eventually calmed him down.

I spent nearly a month in the hospital, as I progressed I was taken under the wing of a physio. She got me into exercises and I spent much of my time throwing a heavy medicine ball against a wall, just to give me back a useful movement of my legs. Her husband was working in Russia and she seldom saw him so I was a welcome guest for tea and sympathy when I eventually got out of the hospital.

Where was I to live? Paul Barnes had got someone to use my room in the flat for two months, I had a scooter parked and locked by Graham somewhere outside the hospital. Paul Polak offered me a room in his house in Ladbroke Grove, not far from my flat. He left a few days before me and I was to go to him. I staggered out of the hospital leaning on Graham's shoulder and somehow managed to ride the scooter with my walking sticks under my arm, weaving my way following his directions and eventually came to a lovely big house in a pretty run down street at the back of Ladbrook Grove.

We were both recovering from operations on our legs and had plenty of time to sit and talk. I had very little money, he said no problem, you talked a lot about food in the hospital, can you cook? Yes I enjoyed cooking. OK you cook, and when you have money, pay me.

I started to really read Chiromancy and got very excited about trying it out. I was now the proud possessor of a straggly beard, reddish with highlights! and long hair.

Paul was practicing again and he had a steady stream of clients coming in for their astrological readings. I wanted to be a palmist. Could I really influence people? Would they believe me? Had I really got any feeling for it? I discussed how I could get clients with Paul, we decided that I should have some sort of form that I could use,

I went to a shop that sold various coloured board and paper and it occurred to me that I could use black paper, smear a white oil based paint on customers hands, take an impression and write my observations with a white pencil on the sheet. That way I could spend plenty of time studying the lines of the hands.

I designed an A4 sheet with characteristics listed across the top. We had worked on a name and 'Professor Bada' came out of our discussions. How can I meet clients?

I wrote to Billy Butlin and requested an interview to discuss a proposition. I had a reply from an underling. Yes, if I presented myself at their offices I might see him if it was interesting enough.

I went to an address near Oxford Circus and met the office manager, he was not impressed with my dress sense or beard. I said I had met Billy Butlin some years before when I had been at Butlins Filey Camp.

The manager asked about my proposition. I outlined my suggestion, I could be their resident palmist and pay Butlins one third of all the money I took whilst working the camps. I described my system of palmistry with my sheets of paper and how I could keep a check on the number I used, so Butlins would have a record of how many hands I read during any one week.

"And how much is that likely to be?" he wanted to know.

I had heard a saying somewhere and I repeated it "How long is a piece of string?"

He wasn't impressed. I said that I could only give an estimate if I knew how many people were at any camp and what proportion of them would have their hands read.

He said, "I don't think Mr Butlin would agree to you covering the camps they are too diverse in many parts of the country. Do you know any of them?"

"Yes, I had worked at Skegness as a photographer before I had discovered my talent for palmistry."

He left me alone and came back about five minutes later, would I come with him, I followed him along a corridor and we entered a room where the great man himself was sitting behind a huge desk.

"What the eff have you come as," he said with a great grin. "So you have met me? I wouldn't know. But, I am intrigued about your idea. We did have a Gipsy Rose Lee there one year, she was mainly reading tarot cards and I believe it may have upset some campers but I will give you a start at Skegness as you know it and if it works I will need other palmists at the other camps. But I warn you, I have built a reputation for giving value for money at all my holiday camps and I need to know how good you are, how reliable, and under no circumstance can you upset even one holiday maker. What is your background?"

I gave him a pretty good outline of my life with a little embellishment, right up to meeting Paul Polak in hospital and through our discussions. I was intrigued with Chiromancy, hence, becoming a palmist, albeit in my very early stages of knowledge.

He said, "How do you see it working? What sort of charges will you make?"

I replied "That as long as I could have an office or an area where I could be seen, I would want a desk or a table and that's all. Some sort of publicity and your main office could keep a check on the number of black sheets I use, so we could arrive at how much I owe the camp. As far as charges, I would suggest that I could do a character study for ten shillings and a study with a forecast one pound."

He said, "Wait a couple of minutes, while I think about it."

I sat and looked out of his window overlooking Oxford Street.

Suddenly he said, with a wicked grin, "I can't see it changing the fortunes of my operation but I see it more as a new interest and intrigue. I tend to visit all the camps on a regular basis unannounced, so I may well show up and ask you to read my palm."

He offered me his hand and said "Go off with Michael now and he will get you to sign up a contract, I will give you a concession until the second week in September providing you don't cause any problems."

"Thank you" I said, "I am sure I will enjoy working at your camp. I certainly did the last time."

I hardly looked at the simple contract which took about five minutes to prepare, I had nearly two weeks to prepare myself before my start. I went out onto Oxford street walking on air. I had met one of the great entrepreneurs of the world and he had been very open and courteous to me.

Maybe being a palmist creates a bit of mystery, maybe this is going to be a real future.

I got back to Paul and he was particularly unexcited. This unsettled me a bit. "Paul it's a start, he saw me, he wanted to know some background to palmistry. I told him what I've read in the book, he seemed to be interested although he did say he couldn't see it making much difference financially, he thought it would add intrigue." I followed this by asking "How did you start?"

Paul had deep set dark eyes and at times he appeared to be almost black around the area where his eyes should be. He also had a habit of suddenly shaking his head from side to side, usually when thinking. I wondered if his clients were put off by this, or perhaps it didn't happen when he was deeply involved with a study.

He grunted and then said, "I started through a love of maths and music, but let's think about how you are going to cope with dozens of people, many knowing each other so you will have to be very careful with what you tell people. I have a very simple book which I found some time ago, its Foulsham's Fortune Teller, and it deals with all the individual star signs and has a rough description of their qualities and outlook, you might like to borrow that initially until you have confidence in yourself."

I thought about this and agreed. "I also need to get my sheets printed, how many should I have initially, I don't suppose it will be easy finding the right sort of printer in Skegness?"

We decided that I should have a thousand printed, he would finance it and I was to pay him back after a month.

The next week was one of frantic reading and rushing around getting everything ready. I also phoned Mandy and pleaded with her to come round one afternoon when Paul was out. She said she couldn't, she was scared of being followed. I, having read a few spy stories, said "It would be fun for you to catch a tube, then double back on yourself and then take a taxi, I will give you the money to cover that, I am longing to see you." She eventually agreed and she came round and we caught up.

CHAPTER 11

The day arrived for me to go to Skegness. I contacted Paul Barnes and asked him to offer my room at the flat for at least four months whilst I was at Skegness. I would go on my scooter I would need a large carrier for my printing and clothes. Would the scooter stand up to a hundred and fifty miles, it also occurred to me that I hadn't arranged for anywhere to live there I should have done that when I was with the manager of Butlins.

I chugged up to Skegness, it took hours and I was very tired when I arrived late afternoon. I pulled up at the holiday camp immediately opposite was a static caravan site, I went into the shop at the entrance and was met by the friendliest of ladies, "I wondered if it would be possible to rent a caravan for few months as I am working at Butlins, and my work demands some solitude."

"What is it you do?" asked Barbara, that was her name.

"I'm a fortune teller – a palm reader."

She thrust out her hand, "Tell me something good."

"You are happily married and you are enjoying life to the full."

"Tell me more, tell me more."

"I could," I said "but I am desperate for somewhere to settle into and relax I've been riding this scooter for what seems like all day."

"If you're taking a van for three months I can let you have a four berth for a reasonable sum, and will you look at my hand now and again."

We settled on my rent and I somehow managed to get everything off my bike and into the van. *So that's what happens to ladies when you say you are a fortune teller.* I thought, *I hope this is going to work...*

The caravan was fine, plenty of room, all the utensils were neatly stacked into a folding arm above the sink and bed, there was a cooker and heater, not that I thought I would need that in the summer. Water was held in a tank just to the rear of my van and I had a wash basin to use. I can be content.

I had a wash then wandered over to the camp. I was met at the gate by a brusque guard who wanted to know what I wanted to enter the camp for, I told him and he telephoned someone who obviously knew I was arriving because after putting down the phone he pointed me in the direction of the management office, where I would meet the camp accountant. The accountant, a mean faced man, made me welcome and said he had been informed about me and he was to see that I had everything I needed. I asked if it was possible to see around the camp, I wanted to see if much had been changed since last year. I also told him I wanted an office or a place to work, somewhere in the public eye, perhaps the ballroom.

"Yes you could have a table in the ballroom in one corner."

"Can I also have a display board to mount my information and any photos that I can have done?"

"Yes I can see to that." He also suggested I meet the head of entertainment as I would be part of their staff.

"Hold on a minute, I am going to be independent of Butlins. I understand I am what's termed as a concession, I am paying you part of my earnings, I don't expect to be a member of staff."

"No I didn't mean you would report to her, she will include you in the 'Who's Who', routine. Anyone that rates as entertainment will be introduced to the holiday makers at the Saturday night introduction meetings so the campers get an idea of what shows there are, and who is featuring."

"That sounds good, so I will get plenty of publicity?"

"Oh, the 'who's who' is headed up by one of our comedians and we have two houses interspersing with the two dinner sittings, all the entertainment redcoats and show people are introduced, we have some music, a bit of mystery and its an hour and a half show to get 'em in the mood to enter all the competitions, knobbly knees, glamourous granny, Miss Butlin, Miss Uk, there are several competitions and their job is to get everyone to feel part of the camp and enjoy it."

"Sounds like that old German expression, You vill enjoy it!"

He took me round the ballroom and we settled on my spot, we went to the dining room, not that I would use that, looked at the swimming pool area, saw the theatre and generally got the feel of the place again.

"I believe you have had some printing done which you will use for the campers to keep."

"Yes I have a thousand A4 sheets in my caravan, I'm staying over at the camp site across the road."

"You're with Barbara and Alan are you, I did have a chalet set aside for you, would you like that?"

"No I would rather be independent."

"The camp isn't full this week but I expect you would like to get started. Will you bring your sheets over tomorrow morning and I will book out however many you want each day."

We ended up in the Ingermelds café and he treated me to a coffee and Lincolnshire bun. So this is living I thought as I went back to my caravan. There was a different guard and he wanted to know who I was and what I was leaving the camp for. So the old story was true, the barbed wire around the camp and the guard at the gate wasn't to deter people from entering, it was to keep the holiday makers in…*phew*…

I was very tentative on my first day. I set up my table in the ballroom and met the head of entertainment – a smiling glamourous lady – we got on immediately. She said there was a Glamourous Granny competition that afternoon in the ballroom so I should get plenty of punters.

"Is that the right word for them do you think?" I asked.

She laughingly shook her head and said, "No it's a term we sometimes use but what would you call them?"

Umm, I was on the spot, didn't want to be stuffy or dry.

"I see them as clients."

"Ok" she said, "I take it you view palm reading very seriously."

"To be honest, they come in a real mixture. You get the very serious ones, the flippant ones, and the tough guy image in front of his mates. You have to treat them all with a modicum of respect and remember that they represent your salary."

I was quoting Paul but she accepted that. I suddenly wanted to start work and see if I could handle the situation.

Then she asked, "Would you be interested in judging some of the competitions? I have my judges for today but we have several during each week and I am always pushing our celebrities into judging."

Hey this could be wonderful publicity for me. "Sure I would be pleased too."

"Ok I will get out the list and bring it round this afternoon and will offer you a selection. You can also appear on 'Who's who', on Saturdays, as we have two shows. You need to talk to Dave Allen he is the compere next Saturday and if you want him to say anything particular about yourself…"

She went off and I took a couple of minutes to contemplate what she had said, so I'm seen as a celebrity…!!

I settled myself in the early afternoon in the almost empty ballroom, as I was putting my only photograph of myself up on what was to be my display board a well-dressed man in a shiny sort of suit came over and introduced himself. It was Joe Daniels, of the 'Hot Shots' fame. "I understand you're using the ballroom as your office, old sourpuss the accountant said you would be here for the season."

"Yes I am, I hope I can get some publicity as to where I am and I guess the dancers at night will see me anyway."

"I'll give you a couple of plugs each evening if you like," he said, "what shall I say about you?"

"Well I guess I'm a serious fortune teller, a palm reader." I was a bit unsure of what he could say. "I work as Professor Bada, palmist to the stars."

He smiled stuck out his hand and said "Tell me something interesting."

I looked at his hand, *better make this good.* "The most obvious thing is your mound of venus." *phew...*

"What's that?"

"Well it's this mound here," I said pointing to the fleshly mound which housed his thumb.

"And what does it mean to me?" he asked.

"Maybe a bit oversexed," I muttered.

He drew himself up a little. "Is it a load of old codswallop or do you really think it has any value?"

I also straightened myself and started mouthing words I had heard Paul say. "I share a house in London with an astrologer, he has a wide circle of clients from all walks of life, some of them won't make any decisions about their careers or everyday life until he helps them with a detailed study of their charts, immediate future and general activities. That's a very serious profession, palm reading is more of a gentle reminder of life and rather than progressing a chart of someone's life, you are actually reacting to the look and feel of a hand. The lines can be interpreted according to Cheiro's lifetimes work." I was getting carried away a bit.

"Hang on a minute" he said. "Your average holiday maker here will be from somewhere in the midlands. It's his one break from work in the year and he will eat and drink himself silly, enter some of the competitions, pick up another holiday maker if he's lucky and have the most romantic time of his life, all found. I don't think he will want some obscure reading about sincerity progress or whatever. Just tell him he's good with the birds and you've won him over."

"Joe, you've got it in one. Thanks, I look forward to hearing your music and meeting up with the band, I would appreciate any help you can give me, I will certainly spend every night here so I should know your numbers by the end of the season."

We parted as friends – I hope. He had been around the music scene for a long time, I felt a bit flattered that he had actually taken the time to talk to me.

I got myself prepared, as there was a competition in the ballroom that afternoon. I thought, I'd better have a sandwich or something before the crowds come. Glamourous Grannies, well that's a new one on me.

Having filled my face with a very ordinary sandwich I got out my roller, my flat board and a sausage shaped roll of cardboard, this would be where my clients would lay their hands so as to get all the lines on my black sheet.

Gradually people started to filter in, one or two came over to my table and looked at my picture and the sheets of paper. The very first palm I read was that of a little lady who was a bag of nerves, she said, "don't tell me anything bad", thrusting out her hand. I explained how I was going to take a copy of her hand, make my observations and she could collect it later this evening. She could keep the reading and perhaps next year she might like to come back and we could discuss what I had forecast.

I thought it was a better method than just reading her hand as she could easily forget what I had told her. She grudgingly accepted that and gave me her hand. I dipped my roller into the paint and covered her hand, then pressed her hand onto the black sheet, checked that I had a good impression and asked her for her name and date of birth. She whispered her birth date, looking round to see if anyone was within earshot. I said "So you are a Taurus. May the 7th." It was a date impressed on my mind from my days in Maida Vale.

"Yes but I'm not very bullish" she smiled.

"Have you had your palm read before?" I asked her.

"Many times but never like this before."

I wiped her hand clean, "Are you a regular at Butlins"

"Yes" she said, "this I my seventh visit, here look I have all seven badges from my holidays." She undid her jacket and pinned across a cardigan she had a line of badges.

"I didn't know they did that," I said.

"Oh yes, I'm very proud of my badges, I love Butlins."

"What do you do in work?" I asked.

She gave a hesitant smile, "I'm a stenographer?"

"Oh," I said, "where do you live?"

"In Leicester."

I was getting desperate to move her on as my table was getting surrounded by people, mainly middle aged women, and a few children with them. "If you come in this evening after seven o'clock I will have prepared your reading, do you want just a character study or that and a future reading?"

"How much is it?" she asked. Pointing at my notice on the table

"Ten shillings for a character study, a pound for that and the future."

"I will take the future. I know my character" she said.

I then had a flurry of people wanting their hands held and taking copies to read. Then just as suddenly everyone wandered off into the centre of the ballroom as the entertainment lady started the Glamourous Granny competition.

Dave Allen was one of the judges and when he had finished with the grannies he came over to my table and we briefly talked about the previous season, "What about photography" he asked.

"I've been inspired to take up palmistry."

He laughed at that and said "I believe you want to be in the 'who's who' next Saturday." As people started to crowd around my table he said, "Lets meet in the Ingermelds café later and talk about it."

I said "Very impressed with the grannies, some of them looked younger than me."

He had a laugh wandered off. I thought about what he had said about my intro, would he say something I thought might be good. *Professor Bada knows more about you then you know yourself* and say *I have an office in the ballroom.*

I had several clients and then realised I must start asking them to collect their readings the next day as I would not get many done before the evening dance started.

I went to the café and after a while when I had started to write up some of my palms Dave walked in, followed by three young kids that were pulling him along with a chain he had around his middle. He said he had been at a kids fancy dress party, and he had been a prisoner, hence the chain. He told them to buzz off and he sat down with me.

"I think you will need to intrigue the campers a bit if you want them to have their hands read," he said.

I told him what my method was so I could get through several people in a short time, showed him one of the prints of palms I had taken, then suggested what I had thought.

"Yes," he said "that's good but what about reading a hand on stage."

"Oh I will have to think about that."

"Or" he said, "You could probably tell someone their birth month."

I said "Let's work on that but I've got some palms to write up as I promised some of them they could collect tonight."

He left me and was immediately grabbed by three women who were sitting across from me.

I thought later that night if we could ascertain the month of anyone then I would be happy to try that but I would need to work out what we or Dave said. It's a long shot to be able to tell everyone their month of birth but maybe a code would do it and I guess it should be with a young girl.

The following Saturday before the show we worked on a code. After Dave had introduced the head of entertainment, some of the redcoats, even a beautiful chalet maid he did a great introduction and described me as a master of observation. "Professor Bada knows more about you than you know yourself".

I was on the stage standing a bit back in my long black coat. He collected one of the young girls that had put up their hand to come on stage. He talked to her and the audience and then she gave me her hand. I was able to inform her of her month of birth. We did this on every time Dave was the compere. When I got back to my desk I had a steady stream of clients, but it gave me some inspiration to develop perhaps reading a hand on stage. I had to talk more with Dave.

During the days that followed I had several people during the afternoons and evening whilst *Joe Daniels and his Hot Shots* entertained. It was interesting to get friendly with the band, all the musicians hated playing for the two afternoon tea dances. They all said, "No musician should play in daylight". Joe gave me several plugs whenever the band was playing and as I got more involved with judging the competitions I found that sometimes I was reading up to one hundred palms, which in turn meant sitting late many nights writing my observations.

I also had a portable little wooden desk made by the camp handyman, which I could take to the entrance to the beach. It was Butlins private beach and all the campers had to go through a little gate, I set up my portable office near the entrance so I was highly visible.

I did get the romantics, glamorous girls wanting to know their chances in the beauty competitions. Even the odd gang – the leader would usually say something like "load of old bollocks". I would smile and ask him if he had the courage to have his hand read. Some got a bit nasty and threatening, so if I persuaded the leader to let me have a glance to see what he was like, they would grudgingly put out a hand. I would usually counter with something on the lines of, "So your women like the tough approach, you should do well with the birds. A very good mound of venus." "Wots that then?" A quick press of the mound below his thumb and a knowing look at his mates would do it. That usually got him interested and he would have a character reading, it also often meant the whole group would then follow and have theirs done. But I had to be careful that my observations were different for each of them.

I had developed a work pattern, starting the day with catching up writing the last few sheets of palms that I hadn't finished at night. Then, depending on which competitions I was judging, what the weather was like and if there was an afternoon tea dance, these would all be fitted in, so I had as much exposure as possible, after all I only really had a five month season and this was my main income for the year.

My caravan across the road from Butlins was a haven most of the time. Sometimes it was a bit stressful getting the readings ready for collection, particularly if people wanted them on the same day. My usual break would be munching my Lincolnshire bun or a sandwich whilst I wrote out my observations. Though I got more involved and proficient there were still some people for whom I found difficulty in producing readings; perhaps it was their attitude or the way they presented themselves, and there were some I would not even try. Maybe I was getting sensitive to people and was concerned with their health or perhaps they were on a different plane to me.

I got to know most of the staff, the redcoats were great fun when they finished working with the campers, I would meet up with Dave Allen for the odd drink and he would come to my caravan some nights, sometimes alone, others with his girlfriend. We did some publicity photos – he was a very funny young man and loved all sorts of humour, he would literally throw himself into entertaining the campers and would do a wonderful tumble act, plus a piano act of dropping the keyboard cover onto his hand and holding it up with a shortened finger. We sometimes played golf on a Saturday afternoon – change over day, often with 'By George' another entertainment redcoat. Dave perfected one piece of business from these, he would bounce a golf ball on stage, palm it and he had a cotton wool ball which he would place on a small tee on the stage and swing his driver a couple of times, then he would announce a prize for the person catching his ball as he drove it at the audience. The audience literally held their breath as he took his swing and the ball would travel about ten to twenty yards into them, the relief was a roar of laughter. As well as being a redcoat he occasionally was a bingo caller. "Extra cash" he said, and they loved him. The camp frequently had big named stars from the comedy theatres, telly wasn't as yet exposing them.

Butlins made sure that everyone had the opportunity to be entertained and most of the campers took every moment to be involved in many ways.

Mandy came up to see me one weekend and we had a joyful reunion, she was perfectly content to be entertained in Butlins as I had got her in as my assistant each day. She also said this will be our last time together. Life went on until the second week of September when the season finished. The work had been very tiring but I had earned good money, had made several friends and I was getting myself ready to carry on palm reading in London but how should I approach it?

CHAPTER 12

I went back to Paul and paid him all that I owed him. I talked to Paul Barnes about my flat and he said that the lodger was very happy to keep the room and would pay me a bit extra to stay there. I also went to the AA and they were happy to take me on again through the winter. I thought with the shifts, it would give me plenty of time to get involved in some form of palmistry.

I met up with Graham again, he had a close friend that lived in Willesden Green and he had a spare bedroom in his flat, if I cooked for him sometimes I could have the room for a song. Berny Dove was a hoot, He was the transport manager of a South African company, he had a big Jaguar and he loved the high life, very often bringing back ladies of the night sometimes they would stay for a day or so. I met two of his friends that had a learner drivers business. Would I be interested in doing some work for them, run the office when they were both out, take on learners etc. "Wait a minute I ride a motorbike, I don't have a car." No problem. One of them, Peter White took me out in his Standard ten with dual controls and said "drive", so I did and after some minutes he said "you're a natural you could give lessons."

So I started working with them when not at the AA. Taking out a learner driver was the most frightening thing a palmist could do and after a few weeks I decided that my life was too stressful. I would try some of the restaurants in London to see if I could interest them in having a palmist on hand to give readings before their clients had their meals. I also met Graham's sister again and started to see her regularly.

I kept up with Peter and helped them out occasionally in their office when I was away from the AA and bought one of his cars, a Standard Super ten. My Vespa had given up the ghost anyway.

One day Berny said his big boss was coming over from South Africa and on one of the nights he would like to entertain him in the flat, would I cook?

"Yes, what would you like?"

"Good steak maybe some little roast potatoes and green beans, smoked salmon first and anything you like for pudding, ice cream would be ok."

The night before his dinner he brought back a very beautiful lady of the night who stayed and when Berny went off to work she sat in the kitchen whilst I planned the meal.

"Are you staying tonight as well?" I asked.

"Yes I'm going to be his girl Friday and maybe have to look after his guests."

That got me thinking but during the afternoon I went in to the shops in the long parade in Willesden Green and bought four pieces of steak and everything else I would need.

Bernie's guest arrived, a large man with a crippling handshake and the three of them went into to sitting room whilst I got the meal ready and called them into the dining room. Bernie had bought a superb grand cru Chablis and I poured this with a flourish as they set about their smoked salmon. I went back into the kitchen and got the huge frying pan and melted some butter, chopped some spring onions and added a tiny bit of madras curry paste to the butter. I fried the steaks – I thought they looked a bit thick but all three had asked for medium rare. I made the plates as attractive as I could with my roast potatoes gleaming. I had opened the claret that Bernie had bought and left them to it.

After a few minutes Berny stormed into the kitchen, "Where the hell did you buy the steaks, they are so tough we can't even cut a bit off them."

"Oh I got them from the butcher with the green door."

He exploded "that's a horse meat place."

I was covered in confusion.

"You must apologize to my boss!"

"No," I said, "I will make you the best omelettes you've ever had."

He was still furious but said, "Hurry up then."

I took all our remaining eggs and put some herbs, mixed into the big pan then crumbled cheese on top of the omelette, put it under the grill for a few seconds then went out and told the boss how sorry I was, I had no idea it was a horse meat place.

I took their plates and put them under the grill to keep the spuds warm and a few minutes later presented them with their omelettes. They all commented on them when I went to collect the plates. They had sunk a bottle of Chablis and a bottle of claret and were all in good spirits when I served an apple crumble with ice cream.

A bit later I saw Bernie's boss go into Bernie's bedroom with the lady of the night, Bernie came into the kitchen and said he was sorry he had blown up but he wanted to impress his boss, and I had rescued the situation and his lady was applying a female touch for him.

The whole evening left me a bit fed up and decided I would find somewhere else to live.

I had met a very good guitarist at the AA and he asked me if I knew a house big enough as he could get 'Antonio and his Spanish Group of dancers' who at the time were playing at a theatre in town. I suggested to Bernie that they could come after their show and we could clear the sitting room, which was huge and had a wood floor. He thought that was a good idea and they came one Saturday night, some twenty of them – three guitars, one male and one female singer. We had the most wonderful party until neighbours banged on the door at three o'clock and said they were calling the police if the music and stomping dancing didn't stop.

But I knew I had to leave Bernie and I thanked him for putting me up. I decided to find a flat in Belsize Park, which I did in the square. I knew it well from knowing Graham's sister, who lived there in what they called the nunnery.

I also decided to do some photography and again did some 'on the knocker' for babies. I tried to sell the idea of palm reading to some of London's leading restaurants but couldn't get any to agree. The winter arrived with my main occupation being at the AA. Then, just before Christmas I got a very exciting offer through Mandy, who was now working for Freddie Laker at British United Airways in Wigmore Street. He wanted a photographer to record the opening of their new office in Dusseldorf. He also needed publicity for their new aircraft which was able to carry cars and would be based at Southend Airport. Stirling Moss was going to drive his car into the aircraft through an opening in the nose.

We, Mandy, a pretty blonde girl named Jill, Doug the MD of the company and Freddie then flew to Ostend to go on to Dusseldorf. We arrived at Ostend and all climbed into Freddie's Rolls Royce. We made good time to Brussels, where he decided we would stop for lunch at his favourite restaurant. I had the most divine chicken curry and I think the wine must have gotten to me as when we were sitting in the back of the car got a bit emotional about it and shed a tear or two which amused the rest of them.

As we got on the outskirts of Dusseldorf Freddie stopped and said, "Will you go into a bar?" He pointed it out to me, "and tell the buxom lady behind the bar that he was in town."

"Sure," I said and climbed out, "but I don't speak any German."

He told me what to say and repeated it a couple of times to make sure I understood. I went to the bar and let myself in and sure enough behind the bar was a very buxom blonde. There were three men sitting on high stools talking and I guess ogling her. I said my piece. "Vollency slafen mit mia." and she burst into laughter and said, "So Freddies in town." *What had I said?*

When I got back to the car I told him she had been very amused by my words, and asked what they meant.

Freddie, with a glint in his eye, said "Will you sleep with me." He was highly amused, I guess this was one of his favourite pastimes as he was a very warm friendly man and obviously enjoyed the odd joke.

We stayed in the Park Hotel and it was a level I was not used too but we had a superb two days there as the office was inaugurated. And I only had to take a few photos as Freddie had also got a local firm to cover the opening.

We left Freddie there and the four of us drove back to Ostend. It was just two days before Christmas. When we got to Ostend there was thick fog and all aircraft were grounded with nothing coming in.

We spent some time looking out at the fog then Doug said, "Hold on, I will get Drunk Dick Smith to fly over and get us." The three of us were somewhat worried by the name, but we all wanted to get back home for Christmas.

We were allowed up to the lookout tower and about half an hour later we heard a bump and an engine screaming and sure enough a few minutes later we saw the very dim lights of an aircraft sitting right below the tower. We got our few belongings and climbed aboard. Within seconds we were climbing up through the fog and suddenly we saw clear skies as we gained height. In no time at all Dick yelled that he was going down. Southend also looked to be covered in fog and mist but he ploughed through it and with a bang we hit the ground. He taxied up, still in thick fog, and dropped us right beside an entrance door, I was mightily relieved to be in one piece and Doug then drove us back to London. Some job ... and I got paid!

CHAPTER 13

I did some more demonstrating for Clare in Selfridges and also worked my shifts at the AA and suddenly it was Butlins time again. I was now an experienced Palmist and knew the ropes; once again I hired a caravan, the same one as I had had the previous year. I was in a fairly happy position financially but nevertheless worked flat out at the camp, again judging many of the competitions, and would read on average about a hundred palms a day. *Joe Daniels and his Hot Shots* were the resident band again. I quickly met up with many of the regulars – some of the redcoats had gone on to greater things, but I was pleased to see Dave Allen there again and we soon got back to our former relationship and he would come out to the caravan some nights with his latest friend and we would sometimes sit up most of the night talking, joking, drinking. I decided I wouldn't always get the palms read on the same day and would often spend the next morning writing up my observations. I still went to the beach with my portable table which I was pleased to see was still in the accounts office.

It was a very good season and I bought some more premium bonds as I still had not got a bank account. Near the end of the season I got very friendly with one of the Show Time dancers, Liz Day. She had a sister that was going out with an engineer from South Africa who had, in partnership with a friend, bought a 48 foot yacht which they wanted to fit out and go big game fishing in the Zambesi. Apparently they had taken their holiday last year on a three week big game fish there and were so impressed they decided to do it themselves as they had amassed money in mining.

As they were so remote in their mine they had to buy everything on tap so they had bought the yacht from an advert in one of the sailing magazines and had got it delivered to Lady Bee Yard in Shoreham. Liz said they wanted a cook crew and wondered if I would be interested as she and her sister had decided to go on the adventure to miss the English winter. I had told her that at one stage in my life I wanted to be a chef, but then I had wanted to be many things. It appealed to me and when I finished the season I went to see Liz at her home near Croydon and we then went to Shoreham with her sister to meet up with the owners. It was a very impressive yacht, white in colour, had twin Volvo engines and towering mast for sail, also plenty of room on deck for sunbathing and eating, I got on immediately with them and Liz's sister Doreen and we all decided that this would be a real adventure and if we got bored I could read their hands each day and forecast the weather. That raised a snigger or two… I had my own bunk with plenty of space, and palm reading wasn't on my agenda just then.

The two engineers, Kevin and Simon, had already listed all their requirements and each day new deliveries were arriving. The three week period of setting up quickly passed and the provisions for food were the last to be delivered so the five of us got ready to set off the next morning, early October.

I hadn't given much thought to safety or how reliable the yacht was. I was just thrilled to be spending a few months in a part of the world I had never given much thought too. Kevin was the more studious of the two and he had acquired some books on the mighty river and the area and also on sailing. Luckily they had both been on several sailing holidays, sometimes as crew, so both of them had said they were proficient.

There were two tall chimneys on either side of the harbour and we set off with a blast on the horn and slowly slid past the two chimneys. Kevin was steering and the rest of us were on deck waving to a few people that had stared at us when the foghorn burped.

We were just getting into open water when a speedboat with *Customs* on the side raced up to us and asked us to stop. Simon dropped anchor – we were still in shallow water. There were three uniformed men on the boat and as it pulled alongside us two of them asked for our tethering rope to be thrown to them and they tied their boat to ours and climbed on board.

We all gathered round them and Kevin asked "What's the trouble?"

The obvious captain said "Well, you never cleared customs before you left."

"Is that necessary? We are going to the Zambesi, why would we need to clear customs?"

"You haven't registered this yacht with us and you must return to the yard and we shall inspect the sea worthiness of it and generally bring you up to date with what's required and then you can be cleared."

"But," said Kevin "when we bought the yacht from the owners we were in South Africa, when we had it delivered to Shoreham we signed all the transfer papers with the previous owners so I can't see why we should be held up by you."

"It's necessary that we inspect the boat now for several reasons and I hope you won't make it difficult for us."

"Ok" said Kevin and as we slowly turned the yacht around the two customs officers stayed on board and their speedboat followed us back in.

Both Kevin and Simon were very fed up and their frustration mounted when the captain said, "We shall inspect the boat tomorrow and will you all please be here. It may take a few days to complete."

With that the two left us and climbed onto their boat.

We all sat around for a little while until Simon offered to make some tea and coffee then said "Let's go into Brighton and have a lunch."

Doreen, Liz's sister, told us she had been quite scared when the customs raced out after us, she was a school teacher and she had never discussed regulations with either of the owners, but she said it made sense to have the yacht inspected as she was certain none of us were smugglers. That caused a laugh, but both the owners seemed quite relaxed now about the delay.

We had a day in Brighton, went to the lanes and ended up having fish and chips with two bottles of wine and we all eventually trooped back to our floating home.

The next morning four men in work clothes came and set about examining the yacht. We were all told to wait on deck as they took various bits of equipment down below and after perhaps half an hour one of them came up and told us that we were very lucky that we had been stopped as the keel of the boat was rotted in several places and would not have been altogether seaworthy. They then did a complete survey and eventually told us that there were several areas in the boats lower quarters that would need renovating and would cost at least some four to six thousand pounds spent before she would pass as seaworthy.

Both Kevin and Simon were really upset at this and asked how long the renovations would take. Several weeks and a place would have to be found that could cater for the repairs. They thanked the four men when they left and after signing various papers then told the men they would have to return to South Africa to raise more capital but we decided to stay on board for a few days to eat the provisions.

Liz and Doreen decided to go back to their home. I stayed with the couple for a few days then we all closed up the yacht. Kevin and Simon had got in touch with the owners of Lady Bee yard and asked them to try to sell the yacht for them. So it was a sad ending to what should have been an exciting adventure.

I went back to London found a bed sitter in Belsize Square, and went back to the AA. I tried to make contact with Clair but he was in Norway for a week, so I decided to do some more 'on the knocker' for children's photos, interspersed with the AA shifts.

The winter passed quickly, mostly working at the AA and some presenting for Clair. I suddenly found it was time to go to Skegness again. It was now 1959 and I had a car that made the journey so much easier. Once again I went back to Barbara and Alan and I had the same four berth caravan, which I noticed had been very much tarted up, I also decided to sell my car as I wouldn't need it for the season.

CHAPTER 14

ACTING?

It was now 1959. After getting involved with Gillette I met up with an actor, Ken Earl who said I must get an agent and he introduced me to his. His agent, and now, my agent, Joan, arranged for me to have several 'glamour' and some serious realistic photos done. Almost immediately she got me a job modelling 'Stephanie Beaumont girdles' – a corset type thing. I had my photo in the *TV Times*, Brian Bada, ex footballer recommends. All my mates mobbed me. I got paid, money for old rope or was it corset?

My very first TV job was in the *Archie Andrews Show*, I was an out of work actor and harangued Dick Emery into giving me a job, "Give us a job sir". Archie was running the show and told me and two other actors also begging for work to quieten down, he would audition us for his programme not Mr Emery. I can't remember much of the programme but found Archie the Dummy fairly intimidating.

I was going up for commercials with some success. My first commercial was as a loving dad with a wife and two kids and I was sickly in bed, taking a lemon based recovery drink – I can't remember the name – but it was in opposition to Lucozade. It was meant to be sparkling. When the director had a bottle opened and poured into a glass it just turned a nasty green and didn't sparkle. After some discussion with the cameraman and producer they suggested they add soluble aspirin to the glass. As it evaporated I was to soulfully drink the potion and remarkably start to recover and smile as my family crowded round my bed. After three takes I began to feel like I would never smile again, but on the fourth the director was happy and said thanks to everyone and disappeared. My acting 'wife' commiserated with me as she could see that I was not feeling very well, and eventually the wholesome potion was left in the gents.

I landed a KitKat commercial as a lorry drivers' mate. We went out to a lay-by on the A40 where we had several shots of the lorry coming to rest and the driver and me were pictured with some anticipation wanting a KitKat break. The next day we were in a studio in Soho doing the close up. The driver, had great difficulty in holding the KitKat bar, breaking it and handing a piece to me within about a 2 inch confine and after several takes the director asked us to swap, could I do it? Five takes later we had it in the can but I had eaten several strips of KitKat and knew it. It gave me a taste for KitKats and I have always loved them.

Then I got an exciting commercial for Guards cigarettes. I was to be a glider pilot. We went out to Dunstable and I climbed into a glider, we took off (I was a hidden passenger) being pulled by a long rope on a machine and after circling round the site with the camera trained on us we landed, I stepped out, took a cigarette out of my pocket, lit it, and started to cough.

Many takes later the director said "You don't smoke do you?"

"Well, not a lot" I admitted.

He thought for moment and said "Step out of the glider, look longingly into the distance and pull out a ciggy."

One take and he was very happy. It ran for months and was my most lucrative commercial.

I also did the very first Strongbow Cider commercial – shot on a barge on the Thames in February. Luckily we had a sunny day but was it cold. I was crew on the barge when the arrow came whistling into the wooden side of the boat and I was prompted to swig a glass of Strongbow. I swigged several glasses during the day as the director kept changing the angle of the arrow and my reaction to it and by the end of the day I was a wreck and it took me two days to recover from the cider impact.

Joan, my Agent, was the best friend of the lady casting Saturday night spectaculars from the Harringey Empire. They were great fun and I met many of the entertainment industry stars, sometimes doing a one liner, sometimes doing something to get my teeth into and sometimes doing walk-on parts.

I was in one when Anthony Newley and Peter Sellers were the stars. We all arrived at Cecil Sharp house near Regents Park to begin rehearsals. It was pouring with rain and no Peter Sellers. We started blocking the main scene, which was to be a gangland meeting and fight between the two star's teams. In the midst of this a small chap arrived in a raincoat, trilby hat and briefcase, he stood just inside the door, looking around until gradually all the cast realised who it was. At first a titter ran around us all then we started laughing.

He just stood there not moving a muscle whilst we were in stitches until the director rushed over and welcomed him. What strength of personality! Peter Sellers was magnificent, he took time to meet us all. I played one of his henchmen – gunman – Plastic Mac. At all the breaks in rehearsal Peter would either get on the drums or play one of the instruments of the Jack Parnalls' resident band.

On another occasion I was in the cast as a cripple in a hospital scene with Morecambe and Wise. Eric had me standing close to him as they did dialogue and he kept kicking my plastered leg and suggesting with a look that I fall down, which I eventually did too much amusement from them both. We then had a St Bernard dog rescue me. I can't think now why it was needed. I liked its handler and got very close to her over several weeks until a male voiced telephone call persuaded me it would be safer not to see her anymore.

Got a small part in *A Town turned to Dust*, the BBC's first western, with Rod Steiger. The director was John Casavettes, who was also playing a leading role. We all lined up to meet the great man at the start of rehearsals and he walked along the line shaking everyones' hand, when he came to me he said,

"I like you boy."

"Why is that Mr Steiger"? I asked.

"Cos you look like me."

When I first got the part I thought a beard would look good in a western and he had a beard and he was also round as I was, having put on some weight. He was deeply into method acting at the time and he stuttered his way through the rehearsals and most of the other actors tended to do the same thing. I remember it well because one of my mates, Bob – a stunt man, had to climb a rope above a fire and as he went up it – the camera rolling – the fire caught the hair on his legs and you could see it burning, the director yelled "keep turning." They kept the camera on him and he ended up in hospital for some time recovering.

I got on very well with several of the actors who were with my agent and decided to form a football team called *Wardour Street Wanderers*. We played in Hyde Park on Sunday mornings, usually against the hotel teams, they were great fun. The football wasn't of the highest standard but it made a great social atmosphere and some pubs around the park benefited from our games.

I was now back in my flat – the two bedroom flat in Ladbroke Grove. Part furnished, it provided a minimum of utensils, a cooker and small fridge that had seen better days and two bedrooms. Paul Barnes, the musician and trumpeter that I had met at Butlins was still there renting the second bedroom. He had an idea which he was trying to sell to the BBC on a radio programme looking at jazz.

Joan Craft was a BBC director and she was doing *The Herries Chronicle*. I was put up for a small part and during its twenty six week run I was in eight of them. I got to know a lot of the cast and made some very good lasting friendships. I was also getting close to one of the make-up girls on the programme. She asked me if I could help her with fixing cupboards in her flat and so armed with a hammer I soon became a temporary resident. She lived in Holland Park just down from the BBC. I did a variety of work including having a good part as a policemen in *The Critical Point* at the BBC, then one day my agent asked me out to lunch at one of the studios to meet an unhappy lady who would like to have her palm read.

I met the well-known lady on a film where she was working with Jayne Mansfield. My agent introduced me. The lady, Lorraine was in an unhappy state. Her husband, a casting director in films, had gone off with one of his 'discoveries'. Lorraine had startling blue eyes, was some years older than me but was susceptible to having her palm read and to being told something comforting. Over a glass or two of wine with our lunch I was quite capable of doing this and then arranged to meet her later, when she had finished the film, at her house in Pimlico for a lunch in return for a good reading.

I rolled up to a very impressive five storied house on Elizabeth Bridge, which she owned. Its fifteen rooms were let as flatlets. She said she had acquired the house through investing her earnings from the various plays and films that she had done in her career, independently of her husband, and it was her safety valve should work dry up. We got along pretty well, we had a long lunch with excellent wines and interspersed with hand holding and some study. I guess my reading was pretty good because somehow I ended up living at the house in my own room, albeit in the basement, and I persuaded her to turn the house into a hotel. I would generally manage it, redecorate it, help sell the rooms and cook breakfasts.

She went along with the idea and initially gave her tenants a month's notice. Some of them left almost immediately. I started decorating the house, painting and paper hanging through the stairwell – all five stories of it. As the rest of the tenants left I redecorated their rooms. Meanwhile I had made contact with a letting and B&B agency to publicise our hotel. After some weeks of backbreaking work, sometimes intermingled with auditions and acting work, I had the hotel 'Bridge House' ready to let. During this time Sunday was our day off and we would entertain friends of hers and some of my acting friends to a good lunch – usually a vast roast of beef. She had the first rotating grill that I had used and she also had good taste in red wine so I was a popular boy and enjoying cooking again.

As we were located within two minutes of Victoria station we very quickly had the "no vacancy" signs up at Bridge House Hotel, and were doing very well. Meanwhile I got a part in a film at Pinewood, *The Valiant*, forecast as up to a week's work.

I had also kept in touch with Paul Barnes, who had taken over my flat in Ladbroke Grove, and the day before I started filming he had an invitation to go to Guildford to meet an old friend and go to a theatre party and would I like to come? Probably having a car helped to get me the invitation. We also asked 'Fido' an old friend of mine who Paul had met when he was living with me in Ladbroke Grove. We were told to be in the pub opposite the theatre after 9.45.

We set off from London in high spirits, meeting up with some famous actors was high on Paul and Fido's must do list. We had settled into the pub which was opposite the old theatre, had a game of bar billiards and were just returning to our seats when a sweater, or was it a blouse? walked in, followed by the most beautiful dark haired young girl. She went to the bar and I asked Paul and Fido if they would like a refill, hardly listening to their reply I swept up to bar about two yards from her. She was gazing around the room and I wondered if this was Paul's friend, she looked at me and I smiled and partially crossed my eyes at her, she smiled back and at that moment another blondish girl walked in and went straight to my beauty. The blonde one pointed at Paul and Fido and they both went over, I quickly followed and we were all introduced. The blonde was Paul's friend, she was the stage manager. My beauty was the lead 'juve' actress in the theatre and they were going to the party.

After a quick drink the five of us piled into my little standard ten and drove off – she somehow managed to be in the front seat. By the time we arrived I knew her name – Mary, and a bit about her and then we spent the whole evening together. I told her everyone else was a shadow, I only had eyes for her but I never told her what I did. The party host had a guitar and at some stage I picked this up started to play my usual three chords and sang a bit to her until one of the chords snapped. I don't think she was too impressed. I fell for her in a big way, her brown eyes had totally captivated me. I drove her home, with my two mates in the back seat, and had a clinging goodnight kiss in the doorway. We exchanged telephone numbers and I said I would write and call her and we would meet the following Saturday, I would come to the theatre and then spend time together after the play.

I travelled back with my mates and talked non-stop about Mary. I knew better than to mention her to Lorraine back at the hotel. I went to Pinewood the next day and hung around waiting for my scenes. I longed to talk to Mary but the mobile telephone had not yet been invented. I was called for my first scene late afternoon, I was Able Seaman Nobby Clark, and it was with John Mills and three other seamen. There was some dialog, John Mills was the hero and we – the rest of the crew, fell in with his ideas. After two takes the scene was in the bag.

On arriving back at the hotel Lorraine snapped that a girl had called asking after me and seemed pretty keen to talk, "I told her where you were and she seemed quite surprised to learn you were an actor. Who is she?"

I could see my dalliance with Lorraine might be on the line so I told her the full story and that I was totally smitten. She was not amused – our relationship, albeit at arms length, was found wanting.

I visited Mary, she was on her way to a Cambridge Ball, which made me a bit miffed, what happened at Cambridge balls? I was restless all weekend until she called me Sunday night to say she missed me.

The hotel was very demanding, I would sometimes sit up till well after midnight waiting for the last guests to arrive and then be up at dawn to cook first breakfasts. My relationship with Lorraine was at arms length and when Mary came to see me it was even more strained. Lorraine had had an affair with John Gilling, film director before I appeared on the scene and he had gone off with someone from one of his films, which accounted for her low self-image when we first met, but they resumed their affair again which was good news for her and for me with my growing love for Mary.

I was finding it tough going at the hotel and one morning I had gotten up at 5.30 to cook the first two breakfasts, other guests filtered down and I was cooking until 8.30. I had just sat down to read the newspaper when Lorraine tottered in to the kitchen and snapped at me. "What are you doing"?

I said "I've been cooking since 5.30 and I need a rest".

We had a heated row in whispers as there were still some guests in the breakfast room. The row grew in intensity until I picked up the empty frying pan and hit her with it – albeit across her behind and said "That's it, I'm leaving."

I went into my bedroom, got my coffee percolator, my very few clothes and my double mattress which I tied on to the top of my standard car and drove up to Hampstead to stay with Clair my Canadian buddy.

CHAPTER 15

I quickly fitted into Clair's way of life, late nights and long lay ins. He was a consultant now with a big USA company that was all about 'Man Management'. He went on programmes initiated by the company and these would last three or four days. He would then analyse the company, the people directly involved with its activities and give it direction ... then he would take time off. His deal with Peachey, the owners of his flat, was that he would totally redecorate it in the first six months with no rent payable. My bedroom window had a short plastic curtain that pulled about a third of the way across, I hung a blanket in the window- it stayed there, day and night. Our life was approaching "artistic". I was trying for any acting work that I could get.

Living with Clair was a hoot. I came in one night to find him sitting on the knee of an immense woman, he curled up with embarrassment and laughed it off introducing me to her, stating she was a wonderful cook and had promised that she would cater for us and see we didn't starve. She had one of her shoes off and it looked big enough to sail to France in it. I excused myself and went to telephone Mary – I was going to Guildford most Saturday nights and she would come back to Hampstead with me to stay over until I drove her back on Monday night. My deal with Clair was that I would get food and cook in return for free living. This suited me well as I would get the odd acting part and did some more photographic work picturing babies, mainly 'on the knocker'. I had also acquired a roulette wheel and we started having gambling parties in our mate's houses that would raise a bit of cash.

One night I had arrived at the flat to find it empty and was about to start making a meal when Clair burst into the room. "Come with me, bring your camera, I have something for you."

"Where are we going?"

"To the pub" he says, and we hurried out to our local. When we got there it was reasonably full in the main bar and Clair pulled me over to the far side where there were four or five fellas, some I knew by sight from my few visits, and a really large blonde woman.

"This is Helda," says Clair, "and she is the world's strongest woman. She has just beaten me in arm wrestling and you know I was Canada's champ."

I couldn't help remembering when he once told me he was Canada's tennis champion and how he arrived on the court his racket was missing several strings. "Mmm, yes" I said, "so what do you want me to do?"

"Well she said she can pick me up and twirl me around her head and I want you to photograph it if she can do it."

Everyone in the bar stopped talking and watched as she sat him on a table, bent alongside it and slid him onto her shoulders, then with a heave she lifted him in her hands and twisted around with him, he was laughing and crying with delight. He had taken his glasses off and tears were running down his cheeks. I took several photos of the performance and when she plonked him down on the table he was beside himself with joy.

"Did you see that? Did you get some good photos? That's incredible."

It was some performance, Clair was about twelve and a half stone and she had handled him like a doll. We were all grinning and enjoying the occasion. Clair bought us all drinks, which was most unlike him as he was usually broke, but it certainly made an impression on my mind. I asked Helda how she'd gotten into lifting and become the world champion. She was a bit evasive but said it had all started in Norway when she worked on a farm and it had just developed from there. She now had an agent who looked after her interests and put her into competitions. She was hardly what one would call attractive, but there was a strong personality there and I imagine woe betide anyone trying to take advantage.

I was starving by this time and my lager had accentuated the hunger so I told Clair I was going back to the flat. I asked if he wanted anything and I told him to get her address and I would send on the piccies.

Another night, fairly late, Clair came back to the flat full of shining love – he had met Fenella Fielding in the bar and she was going to telephone him to arrange a date. He described her in detail to me. I had seen her on the telly and was most impressed with her deep vibrating voice and beauty.

We were at a party in Hampstead one night and I was talking to some of the friends I used to share a flat with when I heard raised voices and then Brenda, one of my old flat mates came over and said, "You better go help your friend, he's got himself into trouble."

I pushed over to where he was and he was being invited outside to settle a difference with a hulking great chap. Apparently Clair had made a pass at someone that turned out to be the hulk's girlfriend and he wanted to 'sort Clair out'.

Several of us trooped out into the back yard and I said to Clair "You're crazy he will kill you.

"Just hang on" said Clair.

So we all get outside. I had become his sort of second and we formed a ring around the two of them.

The big guy says "You've got it coming Yank."

Clair held up his hand and said "Wait a minute, I'm Canadian." and took off his glasses which he handed to me, then put up his fists and turned around from the big guy and said, "Ok where are you, come on then where are you."

Everyone started laughing, even the big guy just stood with his hands on his hips and said, "I can't hit a blind man Yank, and don't ever try it on with my girl again."

But Clair said still facing the wrong way, "I'm not a Yank, I'm Canadian."

We all went back into the party, it was farce.

I was at an actors' party with my lovely Mary, it was in the middle of the equity strike. I hadn't done any work for over a month and I was getting quite excited about asking my lovely if she would like to splice the mainbrace with me. Well I've never thought of it like that, in fact, I thought proposing would hurt my knees and they weren't in good shape. So I could stand up and ask her. I had been introducing her among my Belsize Park mates as my fiancée, but I had very little money and no prospects and she certainly deserved some of that.

I was talking to a producer at the party named Terry, good looking guy with a pretty girlfriend called Nerys, she was a close friend of Mary's and at the time was appearing in *The Liver Birds* on TV. We were discussing money, or the lack of it, prospects and marriage, and that I thought it would be a good lark to get married.

He said "Ice cream. Sell ice cream." He had done it two years previously when out of work and made quite a bit.

"Who?" I asked, as there were two or three vans that would play their music and hawk their wares around London.

"Try Tonibell, they have a good system of self-employment."

After the party and a close encounter with Mary, who was now living in South Kensington, I looked up Tonibell. They had a base in Catford and I was living in Pimlico again. Clair had to leave his flat in Hampstead as he owed the landlords and Lorraine, now very happily ensconced with John – marriage was in the air, offered me one of her rooms in return for cooking the odd breakfast. I telephoned to say I was looking for a job, did they have any vacancies? A bright sounding man named Dave – call me Dave – would see me the next day, Monday, did I have a driving licence – you bet. And a car?

I arrived in Sangley Road Catford and eventually found the entrance. There were probably ten vans in the yard, most of their generators were puffing away and a colourful crew were loading bags of ice cream onto their vans. I went to the main office and asked for Dave.

"He's in the fridge" said a lady with blonde hair. "He should be out in a few minutes".

I sat down in the small office and looked around. There was a calendar with some racy pictures of ladies in various stages of undress, some photos of racing cars and a big notice in red. *All products must be checked with Dave or Jane before being taken out of the fridge.* Jane must be the blonde lady I guessed.

He came out after a while and introduced himself. He didn't have ice on his eyebrows, and he looked warm enough. What sort of work was I looking for he asked, "You sound as if you can speak a bit."

"Well I'm an actor and as we have a strike on at the moment I need some work and money as I want to get hitched."

"This is the place to make some money, and if you are prepared to put in the hours you can make a bomb. You are self-employed, which is a good tax angle. How long do you want to work here?"

"How does that work?" I asked. "The tax angle?"

"I will give you a 'round' in south London, you will go to all the stops on a regular basis. You can build it up into a regular good business and because you are self-employed, its advantageous for tax. But, I would need you for the summer."

I thought about this for a moment, did I want to cart around the same places every day? "Do they work seven days a week?" I asked.

"One or two of them do but they usually take a day off in the week as Saturday and Sunday are the best days."

"Does anyone go on their rounds when they take a day off?"

"Well, no but sometimes I do have people that know their rounds and will stand in. In fact I have been thinking about having a supervisor for each group of six salesmen who could oversee their loading and take their vans out on their days off. You could do that?"

I discussed the pay and he said he would give me an amount, and the rest I could earn when selling on the rounds. I would initially need to go out with my six men, take notes of their route and where their stops were then take over on their days off.

"Give me an estimate of how much I can make?"

"I reckon the best ones earn £70 plus a week in the middle of summer but as its end of April it may take a little while to warm up."

That's proper money I thought, "OK I'll give it a go." I told him where I lived in Pimlico, and my telephone number. "What about today?" I asked.

"Yes you could go out with one of the salesmen, he will no doubt do the round twice in the day, so you could swop at midday with another, that way by the end of the week you will have covered them all. Most of them meet for breakfast in the Brockley Café and we could arrange that as a meeting place."

I agreed and went out with an ex-builder who he told me over an enormous brunch at the Brockley Café, that he had lost his money in a crooked deal and was now trying to make enough to start again. His 'round' included bits of Abbey Wood and Woolwich. Most of the salesmen ate at the café each day before setting off on to their rounds, and the amount they put away would no doubt see them through the day.

We set off and arrived at his first stop, his cow on the front of his van let out a musical bellow and we were in business. This went on for about three hours stopping with the bell ringing. Sometimes mothers and kids came out, sometimes just two or three mums and the odd chap and sometimes no one. He told me the roads we were in and where there were no signs.

He had some fun with some of the wives, and a bit of repartee. I guessed this might be for some, their social for the day. We did the full round, Yes I had made a note of the round. Yes I had a geographers map so it would be easy to follow. Yes I could do this. He showed me how to work the soft ice cream machine. Don't let it freeze up was the most important advice because it took a while to defrost and that meant lost business.

We went back to the Brockley Café. He grumbled a bit as it meant he was losing nearly an hour of selling time but he dropped me there. Dave was there and a couple of drivers and vans – one of which I was to go out with in the afternoon. My new afternoon driver turned out to be an ex-coalman. As we left the café, he was swinging his starting handle and I asked him what was wrong with his van.

"I always keep my starting handle handy in case a competitor has a go at me."

"What do you mean?" I asked.

"Well sometimes if you get to a good stop, before one of the other companies salesmen they might just try to frighten you away."

"Are you serious?"

"It doesn't happen often but you hear of the odd punch up and I make certain I'm prepared."

"Is Peckham rough then?"

I spent three days with what was to be my team, sitting beside the soft ice cream machine whilst it rumbled away. I took notes of all the rounds and their stops. I felt I was ready to go.

On the Thursday I would do my first round and it was in the Peckham, Forest Hill area. Dave took me through the entire procedure. Starting the generator, selecting the hard ice cream blocks that I thought would sell, getting chocolate flakes to put in the soft ice cream – 99's as they were called then, and buying and storing the bags of mix which would go into the soft machine. I also needed cones and a few sandwiches, plus a few oysters – round cones shaped like an oyster. He suggested I bring sandwiches each day as it was not always easy to find a café on some of the rounds and a flask of tea or coffee.

I had to make an arrangement with the driver of each van to ensure that the same level of petrol was in when I had finished the day. *Is this going to be complicated?* I wondered. Dave checked all my products as I took them from the fridge, as he believed most of the salesmen were rogues, and if he didn't watch everything when they were loading up, then they would half-inch a cornet if they could.

I started my rounds and found it wasn't the most difficult thing to do. I chatted up the ladies that came out and nearly all of them asked where the regular driver was, I explained what was happening and they would only see me on good days! I soon got into the swing of things, loading my van in the morning, going to the Brockley café, filling myself with wonderful breakfasts, eggs, bacon, sausage, tomatoes, fried bread, the lot. I did get a bit fed up on some days as Eileen, the owner, would suddenly start sweeping up just as we were about to start breakfast, and when the coalmen came in most of the time they would beat their jacket as they walked through the door sending a shower of coal dust over everything.

I spent a few weeks filling in for 'my men' and got to know some of them really well. I was given advice on how to get blocks of ice cream out of the fridge without Dave or Jane knowing. This was done by stuffing them down your shirt or under your arm as you walked out loaded with mix etc. I was also told where I could buy cornets privately and how to make the mix go much further than it was measured to do – take a couple of flasks of water with you or some bottles and add that to the mix, that way you could make really light ice-creams that looked enormous. And get your own round was the general advice.

I had an amusing experience in Abbey Wood on what was to be my last day on that round. I had pulled up near a school and a lady with two small children came up, "Three cornets please."

"Nine-penny ones" I enquired nodding my head at the kids.

"Nine-penny ones mum, give us nine-penny ones mum!"

I had loaded my mix, well-watered, and was now very adept at pulling down the lever with one hand and dropping and twirling my cornets with the other hand making them look huge, I made all three in one hand and passed them out of my window, I hadn't noticed that there was quite a strong wind blowing and my lovely ice cream blew away leaving me holding three damp looking flat top cornets.

"Incredible" I said, "I can't believe that, I will do the same but give you a flake as well." 99's. I knew the flake would keep the ice cream firm. Same price as a special. They went away quite content.

I talked to Dave and suggested I would like to start my own round nearer London. I knew most of the areas leading up to where I was living in Pimlico. I knew the business and thought I could make more money for me and Tonibell.

He agreed. The summer was drawing near and I could see that stops in the parks in London would be good. I still had a school near Peckham that would always provide good income if the weather in town was bad.

Loaded with plenty of product and having stuffed myself at the Brockley, I set out for London – the area around the Houses of Parliament was always busy. Green Park would be good, Victoria station area was busy. There were endless variations to be tried. I had a tip, that if I saw any policemen approaching, it was wise to beat it.

London was a fairly free and easy place to drive in, light traffic, no yellow lines to deter parking, no traffic wardens. I started plying my trade around where I thought it would be most appreciated. I had two other competitors to contend with – Mr Whippy and Centurian. Mr Whippy had soft ice cream like my own but Centurian was all blocks, which the salesman would cut into wafers and also stick into a cone with a square shape.

I parked just along from the Houses of Parliament on sunny days when there was a queue of people waiting to go in. I also went to Green Park at lunch time which would be crowded with secretaries and clerks, or whatever they were from offices. One day I was working quite a big crowd and a chap at the back started waving his arms and trying to get my attention. "Wait in the queue", I shouted back, he kept agitating and each time I said "Wait your turn", as did a few of the more aggressive clerks.

He eventually got right up in front of me and shouted, "You must move your van."

"Why?"

"You are parked over the central telephone exchange for Buckingham Palace and the phones are going crazy."

I saw two policemen approaching, thanked him and scuttled off.

Mary was at that time in *Twelfth Night* in Regents Park open air theatre. It was her first West End part and she was playing Viola. Having opened at Ludlow in the ruins of the castle, I went up to see its first night and stayed with her until we were evicted by a straightlaced landlady. Ludlow was very interesting and the cast were made very welcome, most of them eating in a super café where the proprietor made a fuss of them all.

I came back and found a flat in Sydenham to be nearer the ice cream place but hated the permanent smell of greens being cooked there so I found a flat in Clarendon St, Pimlico. Michael Winners father was my landlord. He then offered me a small cottage next door which I took on and after we were married lived in it for some time.

Most nights I would finish my round and drive my van over to Regents Park theatre and either stand at the back or go into the food tent which was at that time run by Clement Freud. When the show came down I would often pick up several of the cast in my van and we would drive into the West End to one of the clubs, cow on the front of the van squealing his music, and the actors would be standing up, reeling around as I took corners at high speed. It was a most enlightening time ... and we got engaged during the run of the show.

One day I was getting over confident in my choice of pitches in the West End and was parked in front of the Houses of Parliament when I got my first and only summons. Two policemen strolled out of a gateway and got me. I had gotten used to moving on when I saw any but this time my attention was lacking. One of the cops was a gentle looking mid-thirties man, the other was young, he was ginger headed and wearing little round glasses. The young one said "Right we're doing you."

"Would you like an ice cream?" I asked in my most contrite voice.

"Don't give me that," the young one snarled and got out a book from his chest pocket.

"What's your name and have you got a licence to trade on the streets?"

"I'm sure Tonibell has, but no I've never been given a trading licence."

I looked at the older policeman, "Would you like an ice cream?"

He smiled and said thanks but no he was on duty and he strolled away a bit looking around at a few people that were beginning to watch what was going on.

"Where's your driving licence?" the ginger one asked.

I sighed and went to the front of the van and got out my documents and handed them over to the policeman, winking at a little boy that was trying to get close to buy an ice cream. "I don't think I can sell you one at the moment as this nice man is stopping me." I said.

The little boy turned round to his dad and squawked "The policemen won't let him sell me an ice cream."

The dad took his boy away then as the cop turned to look at the boy. "He won't be selling any all day either if he's not careful."

"Ok, what happens now?"

"You will be sent a notice and a time to get to the Magistrates Court and don't let me catch you around here again."

"Thank you officer and are you sure you wouldn't like a free ice cream?"

"Get lost!" He stormed off, folding his notebook into his top pocket as I climbed into the driving seat and slowly pulled away.

I had to appear in the Westminster Magistrates Court and I got really dressed for the part in my best suit. When I was asked by the leading lady magistrate how I would plead I said in my most contrite voice "Guilty of course. I hadn't realised I was breaking the law. It's my first time and I have just started working in ice cream as I need to earn some money to get married. I do apologize and can assure you that it will not happen again."

A whispered conversation went on between the three on the bench. Then she said "Young man we are all of the opinion that you are speaking truthfully and give you a warning and a five shilling fine."

Phew...

"Thank you your honour." I smiled and went to pay the clerk.

I worked through the summer, lost nearly a stone in weight, earned quite an amount As the weather grew colder I went one day to my school, arriving at the time they would come out, a flurry of snow fell as I waited in my driving seat, my generator throbbing away.

A little chap with glasses came up to my window and tapped on it. I rolled it down and asked him what he would like. "You must be fuckin mad trying to sell ice cream in the snow."

"You're right," I said, shut down the generator and drove straight back to Catford. I told Dave what I had left in stock, asked for a credit and said, "That's it I'm leaving."

"Coming back next summer?" he asked.

CHAPTER 16

I bought a convertible Ford Consul car from my ice cream earnings and did a variety of jobs, some acting, some selling. My Mary, who was then working in Wendy Toye's production of *Virtue in Danger*, a musical of the play *The Relapse*, was given four days off to get wed and have a wee honeymoon. Mary's uncle was captain of the Portsmouth Dockyard so several of us were invited to stay at No1 the dockyard for my stag night, which included several girls – bridesmaids to be, lots of drinking – the Navy can do that, and various games including carpet bowls. Then I was banned to an upper room as Mary and her mother had arrived and wanted their own fun.

We got married in Southsea, the vicar was most impressed with the number of actors in the congregation and after the ceremony appeared with a parrot on his shoulder and did a passable imitation of Hugh Griffiths. The reception was at the officers club. Mary's mother must have worked for months to organise such a brilliant event. Mary had two hundred odd people, relatives and close friends. I had very few there was my Aunt Marian and Uncle Aubrey, best man Alan Woolf and a few other acting mates. When I had to stand up and deliver my address I was quaking but somehow got through it and then we were going to Jersey – the honeymoon island!

We drove off in my yellow consul with some tins clanging from the back bumper – it was pouring with rain. After escaping the well-wishers, I untied the tins getting a bit wet in the process. We set off for Southampton from where would fly to Jersey. The weather deteriorated – the wind increased as we drove the few miles and when we got to the airport we were told that all flights were cancelled. What to do? Mary knew the area and we went to Hambledon, to the *Bugle,* where she had visited with some of her old boyfriends. There were no rooms available, but the barman said there was a new swish hotel just round the corner. Hambledon Manor welcomed us covered in wet confetti, gave us a sumptuous room with beautiful lilies and other flowers and an urn full of biscuits. Then we had a wonderful meal and staggered to bed.

We were married – it was legal! – it was wonderful!. I told her she was so beautiful. I could swim in her eyes. The next morning the wind had died down and we telephoned Southampton Airport to be told we had less than an hour to get our delayed flight. We just made it.

Jersey wasn't too warm. I had hired a soft top two seater sports car and we drove around the island, did some crabbing and a little paddling and at night met various other honeymooners at the Hotels dinner and dances, and we got to know each other in the most pleasant and exciting way.

We came back to our little cottage in Clarendon Street, Pimlico, and Mary went from play to play. She was again working at the Mermaid in a Bernard Miles play, *Eastward*

Ho, then *The Witch of Edmonton*, and was causing quite a stir in the press appearing in a very flimsy night dress each performance. She then went to Windsor with Athene Syler in *Midsomer Mink*. She also did some television, *Sheep In Wolf's Clothing* and a *Top Secret*. She was getting lots of work and doing very well when *Man of the Year* came up with Patricia Routledge, Dennis Quilley, and we discovered that she was pregnant.

I pondered the idea of going back to acting but conceded that Mary was a proper actress. I was just playing at it and I enjoyed earning regular money. My acting career was put on hold and I did various selling jobs through the winter for an Oxford company named Counter Products.

Colin, who I had met at the AA had been left some money and had purchased a restaurant in Kensington, *The Pallette* and he wanted a chef. Because I had lived on and off with him several years before, whilst working at the AA, and part of my rent was cooking for him and two other tenants, he asked me to be his chef. I agreed and he was the first person to import Stella lager in to the UK so the ground floor of our restaurant quickly became a drinking bar. The upstairs had cover for 28 people plus some 30 on the ground floor so it quickly became a flourishing business.

The only drawback was he didn't have an extractor fan in the kitchen and when it was full the place would be a hot bed of smells and steam. I always wore a chefs hat but

I would return to Mary, usually near midnight, smelling of everything that I had cooked. We both loved cribbage and if business was a little slow late at night we would get down to a game. One evening a very attractive lady came in quite late, she said for a snack. Colin said to her "You can have your palm read with your snack."

She said "Well I've just finished a TV programme and would be happy to have a welsh rarebit and coffee but I will pass on the palm reading."

We both talked to her as everyone else was settled. She was one of two sisters 'Four hands on the Piano' act. She was of the Moss Bros family and she started to regularly drop in late at night after her TV performances and fell for Colin. They eventually married but she got him to change his name from Weingot to Wingate, They had two children and eventually split up. Colin, having long ago sold the restaurant, had taken on a house full of deprived people with learning difficulties. I had lasted for three months at the restaurant before I gave in and left.

I had decided to do another summer in ice cream and managed to earn enough to give us a deposit on a house, if we could find one. All our favoured places, Hampstead, Maida Vale, Barnes etc., were very expensive. At the end of the season we went to France and had the most lovely holiday driving our open Ford Consul. We stayed on lakes wherever we could, in our borrowed tent, eventually arriving in the south near Cannes. We found a camp site in Agay and stayed there until our holiday money ran out – some of the time living in the tent interspersed by nights in B&Bs so we could have a bath or shower. We took our time returning and visited several interesting French towns that we had read about. Mary's pregnancy was getting obvious. When we got back we discovered that Mary had high blood pressure and she was taken in to hospital, well in advance of her scheduled time.

I had gone fishing one day with my acting friend Ken Earl and on arriving home found a note on my front door telling me to get to Charing Cross Hospital ASAP... I drove like a maniac, parked my car in front of the hospital and rushed to reception. I was told where to go, ran up the stairs to the second floor and rushed into the ward to see Mary in bed with a host of tubes coming out of just about everywhere. When I came round I had a nurse holding my head out of the window, saying "breathe deeply".

We lost our baby Nicola, she lived for a day. We nearly lost Mary, she was very ill and was under constant supervision for several days. I arranged a funeral – a cremation, and told Mary's mother the date and place ... Streatham Crematorium. I went at the appointed hour and waited outside for Mary's mother. The time of the service arrived and no mother. I then spent the most anguishing time of my life listening to the vicar. I didn't take in a word, I just watched the tiny coffin slip away and I was completely alone in the world. Mary's mother's train had been delayed.

Mary eventually came home and close friends asked us to stay with them in Lee Green, to get over our sadness. Gary and Patricia England, both actors, looked after us and helped with everything possible. We perked up a bit and decided to buy a house there in the development if we could get a mortgage. Lewisham Council were giving 100% mortgages, we could buy a house. We discovered there was a wonderful mix of people from all walks of life also taking advantage of the councils offer.

I went to Copycat selling photocopiers, well, I was going too but Mary got a part in *Robert and Elizabeth*, a new musical, and she would be touring, opening in Leeds. I had only been at the company for a couple of weeks and I asked the sales director if he minded if I had a few of days off to go up to see her first night. He said he did, I had only just started, he didn't like the idea at all, so I said, "Fine I'll leave then, do I get any pay?" I squeezed a few pounds out of him, which just about covered my petrol to Leeds.

I was very proud of my lovely wife as she sang her way through a wonderful colourful musical that had the marvellous June Bronhill, Keith Michel and John Clements as the three leads. Ron Grainer had written the musical score and the director was the lovely Wendy Toye. I became a bit of a stage door Johnny and also went to Manchester when it moved there. I loved it, I eventually saw it about twenty times during Mary's run of over two years in the West End. And I never tired of June's voice soaring through her numbers. But on returning to London I needed work and I read in one of the papers that an American firm was starting up in London and looking for sales executives to launch the company. Tuck Tape, all kinds of adhesives.

I met Ed Cohen the Managing Director for my interview in the Hilton on Park Lane.

"What have you been doing?" he asked

"Well I was an actor until the equity strike and did a variety of television work and a couple of films but since the strike I have been sales supervisor for Tonibell, a big countrywide company and then I followed my wife in a play for a few days."

Ed was a theatre freak, he had seen every musical on Broadway and he would go to see *Robert and Elizabeth*, when it got to the West End – the Lyric theatre was to be its home. Could I get him in for the first night? Could he meet any of the cast? And by the way, you can be one of my five sales executives ...easy...

Four other people passed the acid test, one a salesman, one a gambler, one a worker in party catering – he often worked for royalty, and one an ex-Sellotape sales manager – a Ted Levenson, who knew the trade. Don, one of the guys, was an inveterate gambler and we got along very well. We had some active training on how to sell American style and off we went to the major cities in the UK.

We sold tape to every outlet, particularly the motor trade with masking tape. We couldn't give any delivery date as there was a dockers strike in the good old USA and, according to Ed, who maintained he had flown over some of the docks where our tape was waiting, there were ships loaded down with the stuff. After nearly three weeks of huge sales our team started to get telephone calls in the middle of the night asking, "Hey is that you Don, Mike etc?, you're fired!" I somehow managed to stay put and we opened an office in Liverpool where our first deliveries were due. I went up with Ted and hated the place, he was somewhat older than me and insisted on going to a 'Grab a granny' dance night. Most of the ladies had seen better days and were no spring chickens. I watched with some trepidation and was mightily relieved when it was time to go to my bed. On returning to London I realised I was not cut out to Grab a Granny and I started to scan the papers and was attracted by an advert for sales with a Swedish company starting up in the UK introducing a new concept of communications.

Loud speech. I went to my appointment opposite Victoria Station – close to home! and met Burt, the good looking sales director. Yes I was applying for sales managers position, yes I had plenty of experience and yes I was used to long hours, yes, yes, yes.

He said "I have a few more salesmen to meet but will call you in a day or so to let you know my decision."

"If you are meeting more salesmen, does that mean I got the manager's job?"

He smiled, "That's the attitude I love. Yes you have but it will be supervisory and I expect you to do some selling as well."

I started the very next week. We had a concentrated training period of four days and I was to be sales supervisor but with a patch of my own to work in the city. I would spend two days selling and the other three days accompanying and assisting my salesmen. The loud speech equipment allowed me freedom to astonish potential clients with its method of communicating and as the most advanced one was voice switching, I could demonstrate its potential by standing in a corner of an office with my back to the machine and speak to someone in another office without touching anything.

I quickly got to grips with the equipment and was doing really well selling myself to a variety of outlets, including the major hospitals in the city where voice switching was attractive and readily employed, and at the same time earning an overriding commission on my four salesmen. I thought that it would be a good ploy for the salesmen, including myself, to wear bowler hats. It seemed to work and my team were meeting and exceeding all our targets.

I had one particular experience when I was doing a survey of Kings College hospital to quote them for a complete voice switching system even in the theatres. As I walked around the hospital with the manager of communications making notes of what type of equipment I would suggest and places for the equipment to be situated, we approached one building and as we walked up the steps he said "I hope you are not squeamish, this is the mortuary." As we entered, a man dressed entirely in green with green wellies was coming up to the door with a bucket in his hand that was full of water and bodyparts, and lying right in front of me was a pure white body on a slab. When I woke up I was sitting on the steps outside with an anxious nurse rubbing my hands.

It took a little while for me to gain my composure. I had been knocked out playing football a couple of times but anything remotely concerned with blood and death was a no no for me.

Burt announced one day that Ericsons, also of Sweden, were looking to take us over. We all paraded in our showroom to meet the sales director and his team, which turned out to be him and an accountant. He told us how very successful we were and that with the might of Ericsons behind us we could expect even more success. I was standing next to him, he was quite short and I noticed in his top pocket a comb with hairs in it. I pondered this for a while and when he said he would see us individually in Burt's office to discuss our future packets I went in and said I couldn't work for Ericsons. He and Burt tried various ploys to get me to change my mind but that comb had set me off. How could I respect a sales director with hair in his comb?

CHAPTER 17

I got a small severance and went back to Mary and told her that I was a free agent.

I had a sort of sabbatical, then started a brass rubbing company with Gary Morgan, my garage being the workshop. We hired a dedicated lady who went to many of the churches in Kent and London getting rubbings and we soon had a garage full of mounted brass rubbings. These we found quite hard to sell so I started a company for direct speech and safety equipment, with another ex-salesman of Centrum – Bernard. We called our company JT Electronics and immediately got work, a communication system with an insurance company in Brighton and then a large new hotel in Rochester who wanted communication equipment, possible radio in all rooms plus safety and security equipment.

We fitted out Alice Pollock and her partner Ozzie Clark in Chelsea with a complete system for communication and security, and generally got much work but our views didn't coincide and after some months of high activity we decided to drop it and we shared the spoils. Bernard bought a boat which he moored off Shoreham, I acquired most of the equipment we had in stock.

Bernard and I decided that we would take up fishing seriously, Ken Earl, my old acting mate was keen to join in, he had recently won a *News of the World* competition and had the most beautiful split cane rod. Our first trip was off Folkestone. We had arranged to hire a boat and the owner had said he was aware of the best places to fish offshore. The three of us trundled down and set off. The captain had a young son on board and he said he would help us bait up. After some time the captain stopped the boat – she was about 25 feet long and said we were anchored over a wreck and we should have a good day. As we were all gamblers we decided that we would bet a shilling for every fish, another shilling for every species and another shilling for the biggest catch of the day. We first trawled for mackerel to use as bait and within a short time had several in buckets

Bernard was the first to catch a small cod and I then got a terrific tug on my line and it started to pull, I struggled with it and they all crowded round to see what was happening. I managed to move the fish a bit with letting some line go, then I tightened it and tried to wind in but it seemed locked.

The captain said "Is it live, do you think you have hooked the wreck?"

"No," I said "it definitely moved and it's a bit freer."

I started winding in then got another hard pull on the line. This continued for some minutes and eventually after well over half an hour we saw two great wings of a skate sliding just below the surface, I managed to get it alongside the boat and Ken got the gaff into it. It weighed just over 26 pounds. I was exhausted but triumphant. Ken had yet to catch anything and he was getting desperate, until he suddenly shouted "Get the gaff!" He was trying to bring in something huge, his rod was bent almost double. He started winding in all the time shouting at us to have the gaff ready and after a few minutes the little boy sitting up the front of the boat said "Dad."

"Shut up" said the captain as we watched Ken fight his line, a few minutes later the little boy again said "Dad."

"Keep quiet," shouted his father.

Ken carried on winding in.

"Dad."

"What do you want" snarled the captain.

"Dad the boats turning round."...Ken had hooked the wreck and he was turning the boat, he cut his line and we all had a good laugh, and we started again. During the day we caught well over a hundred fish. I fed the whole of our road with skate that weekend. It constantly slipped out of the fridge when we opened it.

One day Lorraine suddenly made contact. She had married John and they had sold the hotel and bought a farm on the Kent, East Sussex border. Little Broadreed Farm which quickly became known as Little Broadbollocks, via John. She said that when they had bought it, they had acquired a lot of hens and now they were producing many eggs and did I have any ideas about selling them. That appealed to me and we started a company named King Cluck which I thought would make people aware of it. I told Lorraine that the eggs must be free range, with a little bit of shit on some of them, and I would aim to sell them to Harrods, Fortnum and Masons, and Selfridges.

When I telephoned these establishments to make initial contact and arrange to meet to discuss our product, I introduced myself as King Cluck and invariably the purchaser would put their hands over the phone and laughter would erupt, but it did the trick. Lorraine bought a van, she would arrive at our house dressed in a flowing ocelot cape and we would deliver her eggs all carefully laid out in softboard trays.

John's daughter was living with them and was a practiced farmer. She started growing vegetables and I had an idea to sell brussel sprouts still on their stalks, which we did, again to the main three shops. It was becoming quite a business when John's daughter fell out with them both and suddenly left to live with a boyfriend, they quickly decided to sell the farm and move to Spain. Now what was I to do?

I started palm reading again and met The Lady Denise Kilmarnock who was the head of the Red Cross. She asked if I would be prepared to work at all their main functions reading palms and splitting the take with her charity. I said yes, and I did.

Some of the events were magic. Using the best hotels in Park Lane and London. She would bring around the various 'celebrities' for their readings. I used the same method as I had originally when I was at Butlins – painting their hands with an oil based white paint, taking an impression on my black headed paper, give their hand a cursory wipe for the fellas and a long meaningful scrub for the ladies.

One night at the Grosvenor House hotel, I and other concessions, astrologers, engravers and the like, were on the balcony surrounding the great room. Paul Getty was suddenly brought up by Lady Denise and had his done. *What on earth could I tell him?* Mary used to be my dark gypsy helper on some occasions when not working in theatre and this particular night had been to the ladies and on coming back saw that my table was surrounded by people and photographers. She rushed in grabbed the sheet and asked the man for his name and address. Normally I sent the readings to most of them. He gave Mary a withering look and muttered Getty. She was covered in confusion, she had been to his house for a charity when acting in Guildford. Of course, Sutton Place. Film stars, famous theatre actors, comedians.

Another night at a big charity affair a very sombre looking man asked me if the hand indicated obsession or addiction. I said it was quite possible but why the question, he said he had an addiction that caused him some physical pain. I asked him what form did that take, he said his right arm became very stiff and sore when he was involved and I thought *this is a send up*, but no, I asked him what was the addiction.

He said "Salmon fishing, fly fishing."

I asked him how long he had been doing it and he said "Several years, about five years."

"Well you must have got a great deal of satisfaction from that, where do you fish?"

"Mainly in Scotland, on the Tweed or Dee but I've never caught anything."

I laughed but was immediately aware that he was upset with my reaction. I said "I was really laughing with you but that's some dedication, five years. Do you fish with any friends?"

"I used too but because I never had any luck I got very fixated on the sport and I feel better doing it by myself."

I then said "I don't think reading your hand will help. I would just keep on trying but share it with friends, it will happen one day." He thanked me and sauntered off. I thought about it I would have given up after a year so he must be dedicated.

The Red Cross attracted many of the charitable celebrities at that time. It was very exciting and rewarding. I got several invitations to give private readings for the society worthies at that time. Denise often had dinner parties and receptions in her house in Eton Square and I would be invited to read the palms of the wealthy as an added attraction.

I also started working at Raffles restaurant on the Kings Road where a 'palm reading' was included in the dinner, adding £2.00 to the bill. Again this was a good source of introduction to the London scene.

CHAPTER 18

I had an idea for a TV series to be called *Zodiac* and met up with a formidable lady named Norma Corney who was well known at both the BBC and ATV for the productions she had handled. I got financed by an Oil company owner that I knew well and set up a production company aptly named BNK Productions. The B being Brian, K for Kevin who represented Keith Collins, the investor, and Norma.

The format of the show was to be the selection of famous entertainers. The panel of experts – four for each show, would be given the relevant details to help them to make forecasts of who he or she was. There would be a live audience and they could also guess the 'star'. There would be a palm reader and an astrologer as regular experts and a mix of other 'forecasters' each week.

I started looking for my cast of experts and started with a few palmists. The first one I interviewed was living in a council flat in Streatham, he met me at the door. I had briefly described on the telephone what I was looking for. He had dark deep set eyes and I immediately felt uneasy with him. We discussed the programme and he told me of his work, mainly through word of mouth but he did advertise in tarot monthly. I told him I had several other palmists to see before I made up my mind and as I was about to leave I heard a great swishing noise. Looking at him I asked if he had heard it, yes, he said, come with me.

We went into the bathroom and he pulled back the shower curtain and there was a huge snake writhing around in the bath. I hastily backed out and said I would let him know.

I met two or three other palmists but I met one lady who had been to a Red Cross event and she said she had watched me working one night she had done some work on TV and was a natural I eventually found several people that could make up our first trial programme and contracted them for the period of shooting.

Having met several experts in the sciences Mary and I were invited to a way out occult party in Kensington. We took our Volkswagen Camper with the two girls in it, as the party was in a mews, we parked outside the cottage and used our two way intercom that I had acquired from my days with Centrum. A very strange group of people were at the party spread through several floors of the house. The hostess announced that we all had to have our Tarot cards read and both Mary and I stiffened with apprehension – neither of us had much time for the Tarot. My turn came and I thought I might learn something, so I went up some very narrow stairs and emerged into a bedroom with very low lighting and who should be sitting beside a table with a very low light on it but my snake charmer.

He said, "Hello I've got so many to read that we better get straight into it." I hardly listened to any of his patter I was desperate to get away. He turned over various cards and told me what they meant then he dropped one face down, when he picked it up and turned it over it was the hangman.

"Oh" he said, "that's not good news."

I said "I've had enough," and bolted. I told Mary what had happened and she said she would not go to see him, we made an excuse that the girls needed looking after and left.

After several interviews and much planning we invited the lovely funny wonderful Roy Castle to be our first star, and what a star, he was totally accommodating and eager to make the pilot programme work. Derek Griffiths was also invited to do a spot of mime that would appeal to our live audience. Ron Grainer wrote a musical intro for what would be our series. Norma drawing on her vast experience selected a director and with his team they set about constructing the show, a film crew were contracted and we started to put the programme together.

We had an office in Covent Garden, which was fun. As the programme progressed Norma's experience got us our first production making a film of *Applause* for television. Lauren Bacall was the lead star, Larry Haggler was also in it. Mary got a small part. We then made a TV film of John Ogden playing the piano and I thought that we were on our way. We finished the pilot with Roy Castle and now came the job of selling it, which Norma said she would do.

As co-signature on the company cheque book I had been persuaded by Norma to sign several undated cheques which would be for the crew on the films we had made, the stars, the director etc., and she would fill in the necessary details. We had amassed £22,000 in a very short time. Norma disappeared with her son, apparently to

Portugal cleaning out the account. Keith Collins, who had initially financed the company, was all for letting her go but apparently she had also outwitted RCA for a similar amount of money, and they put her behind bars at Holloway. So ended an exciting project.

Mary finished in *Robert and Elizabeth* finding herself three months pregnant, she shared her dressing room with Sheila Gish who was also three months pregnant. Mary did a couple of televisions and she was taken into hospital early as her blood pressure was climbing, and she had Frances/Frankie by caesarean. After a few days we were allowed to take her home. I drove very slowly and carefully avoiding any bumps or holes in the road and we got our little treasure home. After Mary had fed her and we put her to bed, Mary went downstairs and I just stood leaning on her cot looking at her peacefully sleeping and told her just how important she was to us. She must have known and after a few weeks she was able to speak – well she could say 'woof' to everything we told her.

We were becoming very friendly with Kevin Colson, who took over from Keith Michel in *Robert and Elizabeth*. As he was also with me in BNK I was seeing a lot of him and we became regulars at the Knightsbridge Sporting Club. Ann, his wife and Mary were seeing much of each other too and the club laid on many events for their members. The Berkley Square Ball was an annual high spot and I remember carrying Mary to the club's Rolls Royce to be chauffeured home with her calling out for

David Essex who we had recently seen in *Godspell*. Another famous night was seeing Frank Sinatra, but after many a free meal and exciting programmes the club was closed down – apparently there was some illegal goings on.

Mary started going up for plays again and landed the juve lead in John Gielgud's production of *Halfway up the Tree* by Peter Ustinov. At the time her mother was ill with "Asian Flu" and put us off coming to see her in Southsea, she thought she had Asian Flu which was sweeping the country at the time. Mary got worried and decided to rush down by train and help her out and do housework etc. Her mother insisted on driving her to the train station saying she felt like a "Giant Refreshed as a result of the visit".

Mary would phone her each day to see how she was progressing, after some days of not getting an answer to our phone calls we asked the police to check as she was very deaf. Sadly she had died alone. We, with Peter, her brother, arranged the funeral and set about clearing the house and selling it.

We were very settled in Lee Green and had acquired a wonderful Au pair, Collette, a very engaging French girl who was wonderful with Frankie, Mary and me. She called me Monsieur Airy chest and was a ball of fun.

We decided to look at houses in Blackheath and almost every day wherever I was working I would drive through the village and we found a house on the heath, in St Germans Place. It was being built on the old St Germans Chapel which had been demolished by a buzz bomb in the war. We went back to Lee and we weren't totally sure if we wanted to buy it. The next day I went back alone and climbed over the scaffolding. It was a sunny morning I could see about a mile of grass to the west, the sun flooded the garden which overlooked a school playing field. I went to the Agents in Blackheath and agreed to buy it.

CHAPTER 19

Mary had Jess very prematurely and again under a caesarean op. Jess was very small, weighing only five pounds and she was immediately taken to the main unit in Hammersmith. Every day Mary used a pump to produce her milk and I drove it over to Hammersmith and watched this tiny figure in a very small incubator, who didn't appear to be breathing, lie totally still. Jess had contracted Pneumonia at three days and it was touch and go as to whether she would survive. Eventually Mary was considered well enough to leave the hospital and go to Hammersmith, she was shocked to see little Jess lying completely still barely breathing … but after nearly three weeks Jess survived and we were able to take her home with immense joy and gratitude in our hearts.

I saw an advert for a Sussex company, Bradley and Vaughan, who wanted salesmen to sell upmarket property in Spain. I went to Haywards Heath and I got a job selling in the Costa Blanca. Five of us, all new salesmen, were flown out to see where we would be working and to update the sales technique. The company had various property's from Javea to Benidorm. Javea was mainly with plots for villas, and dotted along the coast several other developments of either apartments or villas. Benidorm was overdeveloped even then, we had an apartment block several hundred yards back from the sea. If one hung out on the balcony you could just about see the sea, good selling point.

I quickly settled into my role and followed up leads provided by the company. I met a couple in Bexleyheath, a dentist and his architect wife, who I persuaded to come on my first inspection flight. They fell in love with Javea and I got them to sign a £23,000 deal on a villa, which they would have built. That was a good commission for me. I could see that this could be a very profitable job.

I was following up leads that Bradley and Vaughan provided and started taking clients over every other weekend. One of the other salesman, a Bob Payne, and I became good friends. He was an ex-journalist and had an abiding love of cribbage, so we were easily amused in our spare time. I covered all of South London and Kent, he had North London and Hertfordshire. We suggested to B&V that we could arrange an exhibition in London to sell our Spanish properties, in the Holiday Inn on Edgware road, we thought three days would suffice. We advertised in the then three London evening papers, set it all up with a display of recently taken photos of the property, some overhead projection pictures and waited for the punters to roll in.

We waited, and waited, the first day saw five people, we didn't give them too hard a sell and had a lot of fun describing our properties, particularly the ones in Benidorm with their sea view. The second day no one by mid-afternoon and Bob and I decided to play cards, cribbage, we were both addicts. We had just started and I was facing the door and looking up Mr Vaughan was walking in. I smiled over Bob's shoulder and said "Hello Mr Vaughan."

"Pull the other one" said Bob, shuffling the cards.

"You're very busy I see" said Mr Vaughan.

"It's very quiet," we both admitted. But at that moment in walked a very smartly dressed young man with a big hairstyle, "I saw your advert and thought I would have a look. I'm very interested in Spain."

We gave him the outline of our property locations and started the overhead projector. He followed everything and wanted more. After seeing our promotional film, he asked us about how the business had been set up and said he was interested, could he call me at home later that evening. "Yes I would like to come on a sales weekend."

I took his card and told him I would send him his ticket and instructions.

Mr Vaughan said "I must be good luck," and with that he excused himself saying "I will call you tomorrow to see how you've done."

I looked at our first positive lead, his card said *Montague Howard Property Company, Mr Monty Howard.*

"That's strange," I said to Bob "Why would a property man want to come on an inspection weekend?"

"Maybe he wants to learn something."

"Yeah but doesn't make much sense to me."

"Well call him later on and ask that question."

Another punter came in and was pretty thick, we dealt with him as best but we were on a loser. I did a passable imitation of someone hanging out of a balcony to see the sea in Benidorm which amused Bob, and amid much laughter our man slid out. Then we had a run of punters some serious, others just dipping their toes in the water. It was still early days for overseas property. And most people said they were nervous about buying anything in Spain, The third day however we did get five people to commit to coming on the next inspection flight and in each case we suggested they bring their spouses. We dismantled our exhibition and staggered home.

Later that evening I telephoned Mr Monty Howard – call me Monty, and he was evasive but suggested we meet for lunch the next day as he had a proposition. He told me he was contemplating promoting property development in Nerja, southern Spain. He asked me if I would be the sales manager there for his company, which was based in London, and had a variety of land, villas and apartments in Nerja, Costa del Sol.

The next day we met and he gave me a superb lunch at Simpsons in the Strand. He was starting his own overseas property company and formally offered me the position of sales manager. We would go to the Costa del Sol the next weekend and look at Nerja, he had seen it with his lawyer and wanted to set up an operation there. He wanted an instant decision then he would arrange the flights and hotel. He said I could bring my wife too if she is able. I spelt out my requirements, salary and commissions and he agreed everything. I resigned from Bradley and Vaughan and decided southern Spain might be warmer.

The next weekend we flew to Malaga, hired a car and trundled along the coast road through some very unimpressive building sites and after nearly an hour came to Nerja. We rounded a bend where the mountains sloped down to the sea, and before us was a stretch of green and a small town overshadowed by the most attractive mountain range. It was lovely, we stayed at the Balcon Hotel, on the Balcon de Europa. Nerja is an old Spanish town with all the streets running out from the Balcon in a spiders web of intrigue. The Balcon was the centre for everything in the town, jutting out over the sea, massive palm trees on either side and overlooked by the Almahara mountain range.

We met his potential builder, he had several developments, two large apartment blocks on the sea front, land for a village villa development, odd apartments he was restoring in other blocks. Monty was a brilliant negotiator, a little over generous in some things but he wanted sole representation of the builder – Orpherosa, in the UK. He wanted costs to be shared for producing a booklet on Nerja and the properties for sale. He wanted designers and engineers to be available every other weekend when we would bring down twenty prospective buyers, a bus laid on to meet and greet at Malaga. All the men were to be given a bottle of brandy and the ladies a bunch of flowers. Monty wanted the weekends inspection to be 'Hollywood'. The builder agreed everything.

Nerja was a very interesting place, I named it Cornwall with sunshine, as unlike much of the coast in the Costa del Sol, which has long flat beaches. Nerja had coves and small inlets with a wonderful mountain range behind the town. I completely fell for the town. It had tremendous potential. There were bars with flamenco music, good restaurants, Nerja Caves, sunshine and the wonderful Balcon De Europa, many an hour watching life pass by!

We looked at the prospective apartments on the coast, both blocks were already completed and Orpherosa had started selling to tourists. We looked at the land which could house forty terrace type villas and several three or four bedroom villas, where a pool would be built, and restaurant space available. We then planned places where we could eat each day and a programme that encompassed hard selling.

Each inspection weekend would start at Heathrow on Friday late morning, we would fly by Iberia and the front 25 seats were reserved for our group. We would have French champagne laid on, be met by a bus at Malaga with a charming German young man, Dieter, who would be our guide and translator if required. We would also have a very attractive Swedish girl named Eva - assisting sales. Beer and brandy was served to the men, Cava to the ladies and we would arrive at the Balcon Hotel in a high state of excitement fuelled by unlimited alcohol.

We went back to London very excited by the prospect of the business. We now had to get salesmen, produce adverts in the top three or four newspapers for our property and get up and running. I telephoned Bob, he was just back from the Bradley and Vaughan inspection weekend, none of his prospects had confirmed and he was ready for a change. He agreed to be my first salesman at the same basic and commission rate as he had at B&V. The next two weeks were hectic, we had responses from our advertising, both from potential salesman and interested punters in the upmarket papers, *The Times*, and *Sunday Times*, *The Telegraph* and *Observer*. I was interviewing salesmen during the day and following up leads in the evenings in the greater London area. We produced an attractive brochure using much of Orpherosa's original.

The response was good, we had something to offer the salesman who would all be on commission. After some hectic training and background of Nerja, I then held a sales training programme in offices we had found in Wimbledon, after two days our salesmen were ready to follow up the leads we produced and we quickly filled our twenty places for the first visit.

I wanted the salesmen to get the potential buyers to settle on what they would like before we flew them to Spain from our selection of apartments, villas to be built, and the village already on its way, La Noria. This was about half a mile back from the sea, built in the shadow of the Almahara mountain range that ran along the back of Nerja. These were mainly two bed villas in a terrace, the site had a good sized swimming pool and a restaurant in the middle of the area to be developed.

For our first inspection flight the promotion held up well. We, Monty, me, Bob and Dave Hickson – one of our recruited salesmen, sat in the front row of the economy section and we had 20 punters – nine couples, one lone lady, and one lone man lined up behind us. Once our aircraft levelled off the champagne arrived and everyone, but Bob who was a reformed alcoholic we discovered, sampled it and continued through the flight. We marshalled everyone at Malaga and sure enough our coach was waiting with Dieter, our German helper and the most beautiful Swedish girl, Eva, who proceeded to offer the men their bottles of 103 while Dieter handed out bunches of flowers for the ladies.

Then beer or 103 was offered to everyone and Spanish bubbly for the ladies. I did my Ronny Ronald impressions, whistling. Monty told a couple of stories including the fact that we would terminate at the hotel on the Balcon de Europa where Alphonso the 13th had galloped down through Spain and arriving on the outcrop had said 'This is indeed the Balcony of Europe". Luckily none of our potential clients had been to Nerja so no one could differ. We later found out he actually arrived by car. When we got to the hotel Monty announced that we would meet in an hour at 8.30 for dinner and during that time we would give our plan for the weekend.

Everyone settled into their rooms in the Balcon de Europa hotel, all with balconies overlooking the sea. Our Builder, Orferosa would be at the meeting and that would be followed by dinner in the town at Eva and Mike's restaurant.

I went to my room, opened my door onto the balcony and I was looking out over the Mediterranean. I could hear other voices above and around me as some of our clients marvelled at the view and the hotel. This is romantic I thought, I must bring Mary on the next trip she will love the place.

During dinner some of our clients were beginning to show the effect of the continuous booze offered but generally everyone listened to our planning for Saturday. We had tried to get our clients to specify which development they would favour during our first meetings in England and the four of us took our people to one of the three choices. The two apartment blocks, Acapulco Playa and Torresol were within easy walking distance from the hotel. La Noria, the villa development was about half a mile away on the road to Frigliana. For clients had shown an interest in Orpherosa we had a mini bus we loaded them into. After showing the apartments and confirming the clients interest we were to take them back to the builders offices in the square behind the church, right in the heart of Nerja. In front of the office was a square with three bars and the entire square was taken up with tables and chairs so one could happily sit and watch life go by and also do any dealing with property.

Sales took place Saturday morning, then we had a lunch at Torresol, sitting outside in the winter sun. The afternoon was for more sales presentations then a wonderful dinner at Peperico's.

After a sumptuous dinner we walked everyone ... well those that could still do that, around the town showing them the night spots. There was a particularly good nightclub with dancing just behind the Balcon hotel. The flamenco bar was always a good stop. By midnight most of the punters were ready for bed and we said 8.30 in the morning for breakfast.

Gradually our clients were getting involved and confirming their interest in Opherosa's office. Our first weekend was very successful, by Saturday afternoon six of the couples bought and the lone lady bought, mainly apartments either in Torresol or Acapulco Playa block. Sunday morning we took everyone to the caves, a huge underground theatre like place, in fact as tourism developed in Nerja, major concerts were situated there and one weekend Segovia gave a concert. We then had a light lunch and those that had bought homes were given the afternoon off. The stragglers were taken round the developments again to see if we could convert them. That evening everyone was taken to the lovely Parador for dinner, that set the scene for congratulations from Orpherosa himself to those that had bought and he outlined life in Nerja. His family had been there for several generations and he obviously loved the place, he was also artistic in his descriptions of the mountains, the farmers lives and how Nerja had developed from a small village. I found it fascinating as did most of us there.

The next morning, Monday, the few that had not bought we took to La Noria and another couple confirmed, meanwhile those that had bought were taken to the furniture shop by Dieter so they could see what was available for their apartments.

We all met at Opherosa's office and had a light lunch in the square then our coach arrived and we left. Monty and I, on the way back to Malaga, discussed how the first programme had worked out and we decided that the pattern for the inspection weekends was ok. We were both delighted with the response, most of our clients had bought homes and that was very satisfying.

We practiced the same approach and during nearly two years of working in Nerja we came across some characters and made several lasting friendships.

One week I followed up a lead from a psychologist who was listed in Harley Street in London and at another address in Rye. On telephoning him I asked where he would like to meet me, in London or Rye.

"Neither" he said, "lets meet at Victoria station on Tuesday next at 12.30. Perhaps we can have a spot of lunch together."

Not using Victoria much I asked where. He suggested under the clock in the main area.

"Ok how will I know you?"

"I will be wearing a long black coat, a trilby hat, and carrying a copy of the financial times."

"Ok" I thought about this, sounds a bit like a detective story, cloak and dagger stuff. Where to eat?

I knew a good Italian restaurant just back from the station where I had eaten with my oil company friends. I booked a table.

I went to Victoria station and sure enough under the clock was someone with a flowing cloak, dark glasses, huge trilby hat and he was scanning a paper, as I got nearer it was pink the *Financial Times*. This could be fun! I introduced myself and he said, "I am pleased to meet you my man. Have you booked a decent restaurant?"

"Italian" I said, "Its good I've eaten there before."

"Very good, we will discuss our property investment over a good lunch with perhaps a serious bottle of wine?"

As we walked towards the restaurant I said, "I must tell you, we make quite a heavy investment on all our prospective clients and normally we meet in their houses, this is unusual to spend a lot on entertaining unless of course you do intend to come to Nerja. Then I am happy to share a lunch with you" Will he notice the share I thought.

"My good man after I saw your advertisement I researched Nerja, and whilst it is east of Malaga, therefore reasonably untouched by tourism. It does sound very interesting so yes, you have my word as a gentleman that I will be on the next inspection flight with you. I will also show you a bank statement so you can see I am a man of means."

This is getting farcical, I thought, but if he's as good as his word, he might make the weekend interesting as he was obviously a few coppers short of a pound.

We arrived at the restaurant and he carefully took off his cloak and asked the lingering young girl to put it on a coat hanger, his trilby was also to be taken care of.

We sat down, there were a few other clients but almost as soon as we scanned the menu, in came a friend – a very successful Oilman, the chairman of a major company that I knew very well as his daughter and her acting husband were close friends of ours. We often went to Worthing for weekends of snooker, games, drinking and fun where he had a very big house. Keith had his wife, both daughters, and one other a young Italian man that was courting the other daughter. I stood up and gave the ladies a kiss and a high five with Keith as they went on to their table.

"Introduce me," my client said.

"Why do you want to meet them?"

"I think you should introduce me", and with that he leapt up and walked over to their table. He was going round shaking hands with them all. Keith being Australian and pretty blunt said, "What's all this about, we don't know you?"

"Ah", he says "I am an investor with your friend Brian he thought you might like to meet me."

"Let's wait till after lunch" Keith almost snarled, giving me a wink.

"Come on back to our table Phillip." I led him back, he was now quite excited and asked me who they were.

I explained my relationship with them, "Keith backed me in a television production company earlier, he is a fantastic man who had been very successful in the Middle East after the war, and eventually found his way into the oil industry where he was now a big force in exploration. One of his daughters, Anne, is a close friend of ours, she is a photographer and model, and her husband is a well-known actor. The other daughter, the very beautiful dark one over there is a film star in Italy and the smooth looking guy with her is also an Italian actor. I don't know him, I think they very recently met on a film in Rome. There you have it. But let's get back to why we are here."

He kept looking at them all hoping I guess, for a glance but they were all deep into their menus apart from Keith who was in conversation with the manager of the restaurant, nodding in our direction. A few minutes later two glasses of champagne arrived at our table and I gave a single clap of my hands and raised my glass to Keith. Phillip was straining to go over and thank him but I told him we must leave them in peace.

I explained the weekend inspection routine and asked what sort of property he was interested in. I asked if he would be bringing a wife or partner, to which he replied that he lived with his mother in Rye when not practicing in Harley Street.

"Will you bring your mother?"

"No she is partially invalided and would not be up to the rigours of a flight and high living weekend."

But, he insisted, he was interested in buying something that had the possibility of getting a wheelchair into the property.

"Ah you would be better with one of our La Noria properties", and with that I got out my presentation book with photos of the nearly completed first row of two bedroom semi-detached villas.

He took a passing interest but for now wanted to eat, as he was starving he said. "I left Rye early this morning as I had a suit fitting in Saville Row and didn't want to be late for our appointment."

He started waving his menu and the maitre de came over.

"What are you recommending my good man" he said.

I tried to not be there.

The maitre de gave him a steady appraisal and asked, "Are you a fish, meat, or pasta man?"

"All of those" he says.

"Well our calves liver is the best in London"

"Thank you. I love calves liver, can I have it just under medium rare, perhaps just pink, I eat in some of the best restaurants in the world so I shall study your recommendation closely."

"I will join him please, medium rare" I mutter.

"Wine list please." he asked.

"Hold on a minute Phillip I believe I am taking you for this lunch, I will select the wine." I know that the wine list is extensive and some of the wines are very expensive. "I think to complement the liver we will have a Barola."

"Excellent choice" he said, and started to look around the restaurant.

I eventually get him to look at some of the publicity leaflets I have and the food arrived. He was completely happy and took tiny sips of his wine nodding reverently as he did so. I told him more about Nerja as we ate. He wanted a tiramisu which we both had, he was still only sipping his wine and I guess out of the bottle I have drunk three-quarters of it. We have a calm moment or two and after coffee Phillip wanted to go over to give Keith one of his cards. I told him it would not be well received and now asked him to confirm his visit to Nerja the following weekend by giving me the thirty pounds which we charged for the inspection flight, which I stressed was returned and included in the cost price if he buys a property.

"That's perfectly understood" he said whipping out a bank statement which he thrusted into my hand. "You can see I am a man of means" he said.

The bank statement showed over thirty three thousand pounds at the bottom of the list, he was about to take it back when I noticed the date. It was March 1959. "That's a bit out of date Phillip." I said.

"My dear fellow I must have brought the wrong one, how could I have made such a dreadful mistake. I don't have a cheque book on me but you can rest assured that I am a man of my word and a cheque will be winging its way to you tonight when I get back to Rye."

I gave him the registration form and pointed out what was required and where to fill in all his details including the cheque. As we were about to leave he scurried over to Keith's table again and bowing low to the ladies waved his trilby in an elegant gesture and told them how charmed he was to meet them and hoped to see them again.

I left him at Victoria station and as I caught my train to Blackheath I thought, what a waste of time and money, and I must telephone Keith and Anne to apologize for him.

I arranged over the telephone for a lady from Great Yarmouth to be on the next weekend flight, in her case I didn't go to see her in her hotel but we discussed Nerja and what we had to offer. She was very interested because as she said, Great Yarmouth was fine when the weather was good and it was warm but most of the time it was very raw and she desperately wanted some sun now and again.

I was most surprised when the next day I got a thirty pound cheque from Phillip and a letter thanking me for my hospitality and that he would be taking to Nerja some of his testing equipment that he used on clients with general psychotic problems as he wanted to help people in life. I went to Canterbury following another lead and booked another couple – our other salesmen had converted six couples and two single women to come so we had our full complement of seats filled.

Friday arrived and my Great Yarmouth lady had telephoned to say she was about to be on her way and was there anywhere around where I live that she could park as she was wary of driving in to London and didn't like the charges at Heathrow. I gave her directions and told her she could park at the rear of my house for the weekend. She arrived in a gleaming Jaguar car. She was probably in her forties and obviously used to getting her own way in life. I had already loaded my Volkswagen Camper with my own case and we added hers and set off for the Charing Cross Thistle hotel where we were to meet Phillip. She told me as we drove up the old Kent road that she used to work in London several years ago when she had a catering business and had at one stage catered for Buckingham Palace.

Phillip had two cases and was sitting just inside the hotel surrounded by newspapers. I help him load and asked why the two cases for a weekend visit.

"My dear fellow I will need a change of clothing for each day and I have brought my dinner suit for Saturday evening and I also have my test equipment."

I introduced him to Zelda my Great Yarmouth lady as he climbed in. He sat beside her and prattled away for the whole journey.

I dropped them of and went to park. Monty was waiting at the entrance and he greeted them both and took them through to the Iberia lounge, which we had now included on our programme.

I had warned him that Phillip would probably make life a bit difficult for us but just to tolerate him. On joining them Zelda came up to me and asked if I please ensure that she was well separated from Phillip as he was upsetting her.

We got our call and our bags were transported through the check-in desk and as we were ferried onto the aircraft, I tried to allocate the seating, everyone accepted this and I breathed a sigh of relief. I had put Phillip next to a couple from Cardiff and the man was a born joker.

Monty, me, and our two salesmen sat in the front row and the others made themselves comfortable as we waited to take off. Suddenly I heard an exasperated snarl from behind. Zelda was sitting on the outside of her row and Phillip had gotten up from the row behind her and was trying to tell her how to fix her safety belt and had spilt some orange drink over her legs.

I undid my belt and pushed Phillip back into his seat, asking Colin the Cardiff man to keep an eye on him.

Nothing of great importance happened during the flight, we quaffed our French champagne and I could hear Phillips voice talking the whole time. I played a couple of games of crib with Bob and we arrived at a sun filled Malaga.

Our coach was waiting with Dieter and Eva, Phillip immediately sat alongside Eva and was plying her with questions. Dieter had acquired some scampi which he served with the wine that he brought. I heard Phillip telling Eva to eat the whole seafood as the roughage was good for you. He was there with bits of scampi skin hanging from his mouth and generally looked a mess. Eva was starting to look around with a hint of desperation for a saviour and Bob came to her rescue suggesting she should talk to the ladies as we drove, she slipped past Phillip who now looked around for another victim.

Monty suggested I do my Ronny Ronald whistling entertainment and then we could all sing. But Phillip suddenly stood at the front of the coach and stated that he was an eminent psychologist and he would gladly give us all a free examination of our health and mind when we arrive at the hotel. I told him that wouldn't be possible as we would have a drinks reception and dinner by which time it would be bedtime. He said then Sunday afternoon I will help you all.

We sold to everyone on the trip except Phillip, he told us he had to check with his mother before committing himself and no amount of pressure would move him. On Sunday early evening he was sitting outside the Balcony Hotel with a table full of instruments ready to test anyone that was interested. Bob took him on first of all and ended his reading in fits of laughter. One or two of the clients appeased him by letting him take their blood pressure and let him do little tests on their reflexes, some questions about their attitudes and reactions had to be written down and it all became a hoot.

I wasn't looking forward to taking Phillip back but we did, I protected Zelda as best as I could but it was with some relief that I left him at Charing Cross. He said he would discuss purchasing one of the La Noria Villas with his mother. I thought I had seen the last of him.

Two weeks later Monty stayed at home and left the programme to me, we had our normal flight, reception and dinner and I had two new salesmen. I was explaining how the weekend would go and I was standing out on the very front edge of the Balcon late Friday night with Bob and the new men when two army trucks rushed up to us and several armed soldiers leapt out and surrounded us with guns pointing. I raised my hands and tried in my very limited Spanish that we were at the hotel and were in the property business. We were marched to the hotel entrance and one of the porters came out to see what the fuss was about and I asked him to explain who we were. Which he did and begrudgingly the soldiers lowered their rifles and pushed us into the hotel. I asked the porter what was that all about. He said it was probably something to do with some drug runners apparently landing somewhere along the coast that night and many of the army were watching the whole coastline and were going to give them a hot reception. They didn't want them to be put off by seeing a group late at night looking out to sea.

Our business flourished, every other weekend we filled our allocation of seats and we had over 70% conversions. Whilst it was very demanding and meant I usually worked six days a week, sometimes seven and I missed my family a lot, I was earning very good money. When we started the operation there was a 'dollar premium' on any overseas property expenditure of about 12%. Harold Wilson's government suddenly increased this to 100% and at the same time announced that there would be a limit on anyone spending abroad. Holidays would have an allowance of £250.00.

Sales immediately dried up. One or two had put deposits on property and asked for their money back. Totally understandable as it meant double the cost we had been quoting. I had one particular client who had been keen to build a penthouse on top of Torresol block. He had given me £1500 pounds as his deposit and I had the foresight to get his contract with the builder without actually handing over the money... perhaps it was my intuition working.

Two weeks later we cancelled all further dealings with Orferosa and Spain. I played golf with Berry, my client, and halfway round the course I told him I had an envelope for him, his quizzical face shone with anticipation, what could you have for me? I got the envelope out from my golf bag and handed it to him, he looked at me and started tearing it open. "My Dear fellow he said its money."

"It's yours Berry, I felt that the business was about to go under and Harold Wilson gave it a push, I got your contract from Orferosa but never gave him this deposit."

He was overjoyed and promised me he would do all he could to help me as I was now unemployed. He also bought me a sweater in the pro's shop as the one I was wearing didn't meet with Roehamptons quality!

We finished our golf and he bought a bottle of champagne and the very best lunch at the Roehampton golf club. He said "Brian I will at some stage repay you for what you have done."

"There's no need Berry."

But he insisted that he was involved in many things and would keep his word.

CHAPTER 20

I wondered what I would do next. I was owed some money from the sales I had made but had to write that off as did Monty, the business had suffered over the last month. I started scanning the papers and found an interesting ad for a sales manager in humidifiers. Selling water to the brits I thought.

I went to Bromley and met a suave Swiss gentlemen who, after a lengthy discussion, offered me the post of sales development manager with a plan to develop a team of salesmen throughout the country. He was starting an extensive advertising campaign which would provide leads for the salesmen. He was convinced that with more central heating being sold there was a very good potential market for humidifiers in the home and in business, particularly in the printing trade – he already had a salesman covering this. He wanted me to set up a sales agency covering the UK – he would advertise in the best papers and we would all be filthy rich. He gave me a two litre Ford car and offered bonuses on all sales but told me he was a demanding man who had made a major investment in this business and would do all in his power to help me make the sales work.

Very soon I was doing a weekly training day for up to ten salesmen. Leads were pouring in from the advertising campaign. It was all going very well and I soon had some forty sales agents around the country. They were all getting leads and sales were growing.

I quickly prepared a fine sales patter on why a humidifier was essential in the home particularly in the winter. The salesmen would be on commission, as we would provide them with leads, they would need to buy a demonstration humidifier.

Each morning I would take into the office a dried up carrot or sometimes some dried cracked wood and when opening my day I would ask how many of them had a piano.

"What do you treat it with?" Sometimes I received dumb looks and sometimes I got "What do you mean?"

"You all have furniture, do you study it? Are there cracks in it?" Holding up the carrot, "I suggest we all have vegetables in our kitchens and many of them look like this."

"What's this?"

"It's a carrot", would come from one of them.

"What do you notice about the carrot?"

"Looks a bit withered."

"Yes it is why? Because its been in a shelf in a room for three days without the benefit of a humidifier because our houses are too dry, we need moisture, particularly with pianos, sideboards, and veneered furniture, picture frames, I can go on but you see this?" I would pull out a swing hygrometer, and a little ruler. "I will take the relative humidity in this room and it will be correct because as no doubt you will have seen, there is a Swiss humidifier in the corner and it is gently adding moisture to the atmosphere, you can probably breathe better here than you do in say your car or at home, Yes?"

I would start off with the windows closed and the heat turned up, wait until they were all taking off jackets or in some cases pullovers and then turn off the heat and open the windows wide. Meanwhile I would start with a description of each of the humidifiers and what they did. How they worked and their capacity. Look at a grand piano, for older ones without humidification the veneer will start to lift, the legs will dry out! Do you know that all art galleries will soon be fitted with humidifiers, paintings particularly the old ones will see the frames twisting and the paint beginning to line. I would go on in that vein until I had them itching to buy one as a demo kit.

I soon had a team of salesmen covering the country and some of the more affluent enquiries I would visit myself in London. We also had a system for printing works and I would use a sword hygrometer to test the moisture level in large volumes of printing paper. And recommend our jet system.

I did some selling myself in London and one day I was called to Golders Green to a musician – she was worried about her piano. She already had a humidifier which she had bought at one of the department stores but it didn't seem to make much difference. I sold her a high output humidifier and left. She telephoned the next afternoon to say it had been delivered in the morning and the delivery man had shown her how to make it function but the house was dripping with water everywhere – she could hardly see out of her windows they were so steamed up. What about the piano I asked – that's fine I think, well turn down the output of the humidifier and you should be ok. I was tickled by the idea of water running down all the surfaces but I didn't hear any more from her so I guess it worked.

I was getting tired of humidifiers and the Swiss owner, he was didactic and at times unbearable with threats to some of the salesmen when complaints came in following some troubles with the larger humidifiers. I started to look at the ads again, particularly when I heard that Roger Cook of the BBC was trying to interview the directors for some mishandling of customers. Then one afternoon I was sitting in my office gorging myself with chocolates through boredom, and talking to a salesman in Stratford when my line went dead and a few seconds later our receptionist, heavily pregnant, ran into my room crying. She was followed by a man who came right up to me and said "Don't try to move anything in this office."

I stood up, "What the hell are playing at and what have you done to this girl?"

"Sit down and listen, we are the VAT people, I want to and am going to look through your order book and check everything you have here."

"What's this all about, you've upset our receptionist and in case you're blind she is heavily pregnant."

"We are searching the complete premises including the workshop. Are you in charge?"

"I'm the sales manager. If you want the director he is having lunch with his secretary."

"When will he be back?"

"I dunno probably within the hour."

I sat Jane down and told the VAT man to apologize for upsetting her.

"There's no need for that," he said "if you're the sales manager I want to see a record of all your sales now."

"I think I will finish my sandwich first before I do anything else and why can't we have our telephones operating?"

"You are under suspicion for illegal trading and as far as we are concerned all business activities stop until we know what your state of VAT is. Do you take work home?"

"I have some stuff at home but it's of no importance."

"We will see about that after we have seen your director, we will come to your home with you and see what you have that's relevant to this company."

"Are you sure you're in the right country, we had a war to deal with people like you."

"Less of it. What's your name?"

I told him.

"Your address?"

I consoled our girl and told her to go home and forget everything and I would take care of it. Apparently she had been sitting by the entrance and a young man had leapt straight through her open window into her office and pulled out all the telephone plugs, which was when she, terrified, had run to my office.

As I was the only responsible person in the office I was asked to telephone the directors and get them to come in.

"I don't have their home numbers."

"That's Ok we know where your main man lives, he is being contacted."

"I don't like your heavy handed approach to this" I said to an older man,

"It's not your problem", he said.

One of my part time secretary's came rushing in to my office, she pulled up with a gasp when she saw Jane sitting at my desk still wiping tears away. "What's happening? There's a man out there who says the company is being raided and he wanted to know who I was and what I do?"

"They're very friendly vat men and they are waiting for Felix to give him the once over, they are about to search my room and no doubt steal my bar of Cadbury's that's in my top drawer."

I got out the monthly sheets listing sales targets, sales, potential sales and the number of products we carried.

The lead VAT man scanned my book, "Have you sold anything to Seapalm company?"

"That doesn't ring a bell with me," I said. "What do they do?"

"Mainly in the printing trade," he said

"You want to talk to our print salesman, he's out on an appointment."

"When will he be back?"

"I don't know, he's independent of me, I look after the home domestic trade."

The questions went on, he studied the names of my agents and wanted a copy of their addresses. Felix came back and was in a foul mood in which he blasted the furtiveness of the VAT men. There were three of them and when we went into the boardroom, Felix insisted on our telephone being reconnected and asked them to produce any evidence of mistreatment by our company. They grudgingly admitted that they had been tipped off that our company was trading illegally and not claiming VAT on our sales. The telephone was re-established and all three secretaries were now back in the office.

The lead man said he wanted to come to my home to see any material. Felix asked him and me what I had. "I keep a copy of all the salesmen's telephones numbers at home should I need to contact them after hours, that's all I have."

"No matter", the vat man said "I'm coming with you."

Which one of them did and looked through the house. I had a desk on the top floor which he searched through and I said, "You happy in your job? I'm going to publicise this attack on my privacy and I'd like you to leave now."

My wife was about to go out to work, she had been horrified when I told her what had happened.

The whole episode disturbed me. Were we avoiding vat? What was the reason for the attack?

I asked Felix the next day. I said I was concerned that we had been targeted and he guessed that Seapalm were responsible as he had had a bit of conflict with them over the system that our print salesmen had promised, and the system was not working effectively. It was nothing for me to be concerned about. Felix did raise a letter for all staff that we had to be wary of what we were doing, we had to conserve paper, we had to be on time at the office, he was thinking of time clocks to record our hours, the instructions went on and on. I suddenly had had enough of being shut in an office in Bromley.

Because of my boredom I started telephoning friends with outlandish suggestions, One couple we knew well had just told us they were going to Buckingham Palace to a garden party. A couple of days before their visit I telephoned Herb, an American friend who was a theatre buff, and had his own conference and promotions company. I adopted my soft voice and when he picked up the phone I said, "Could I speak with Mr Kanzell please."

"Who is this" he said

"I am the equerry to the queen and I understand you and your wife are guests at the garden party on Thursday."

"Yes", he said "we are very much looking forward to it."

"Well will you be driving your car or coming by taxi?"

"We shall be coming by taxi." he said,

"You will be dropped outside the entrance and no doubt there will be a queue waiting to enter, please join the queue."

"Thank you" said Herb, and I then added, "Perhaps you have seen the weather forecast? As we get special treatment to enable us to ensure that guests get the most enjoyment from their visit, there is a strong possibility of some rain on Thursday."

"Thank you" said Herb.

"We are suggesting that all the guests bring an umbrella and if they could be uniform that would be appreciated by the queen. For this party we have settled on a black and white umbrella, so if you could ensure you have one just in case."

"Oh" said Herb "I will get my wife to organise that."

"There are other areas of protocol which you should be aware of, whatever the situation, don't push or jostle the Queen."

"Oh, we wouldn't think of that," said Herb.

"Well, all I can wish is that you enjoy your day. You sound as if you are from North America is that correct?"

"Yes I'm from Brooklyn and have been here a while now."

"The only other advice I can give you is that when you leave the palace will you please acknowledge the flag that flies over the palace by bowing to it and if your wife will curtsy that would be very good, so thank you for your time and enjoy the occasion."

I hung up and creased myself with laughing and Mary, who had listened to some of it said you must phone him back and let him know it was a leg pull. No I will do that tomorrow night before they go to the party.

The following evening I telephoned Herb and Barbara and said we were having a party in a month's time, gave him the date and had a general chat about things. At the end I said, "Hey are you going to the Palace tomorrow?"

I sensed a pause, "Yes" he said.

"You better take an umbrella cos its likely to rain."

"You dog," he said, "It was you. Barbara has spent the day trying to find a black and white umbrella and she's been practicing curtsying, jeeze." We both laughed, "That was a great leg pull, bowing to the flag curtsying, we thought that was a bit over the top."

Flushed with success I telephoned our neighbours who were sailing to Santander on SS *Patricia* at the weekend. I got Leonore, when she answered I asked if I had the correct telephone number and if she was going to Spain at the weekend, "Yes she was."

"Well I am the purser of SS *Patricia* and I have a few points to discuss. We have had a small fire on the ship and at present we are a little short of pillow cases, we wondered if it would be possible for her to bring two for herself and husband."

"Oh" she said "I suppose I could arrange that."

"Many thanks," I said, "and would it be possible to perhaps also bring two pillows?"

"This is most unusual. But yes providing we can take them with us when we get there."

"Of course you can. We are most grateful for your consideration, and I'm sure you will enjoy your trip, the weather forecast is good. Are you touring Spain?"

"No we are going to Pau and we thought this would be a good opportunity to see some of the countryside."

"Well you have been very kind. Could I ask you one more small favour to ensure your journey will be comfortable, would it be possible to bring two single blankets as you have a twin room on the ship."

She reacted strongly and said "This is just ridiculous, speak to my husband."

Duncan came on to the phone and shouted "We are first class passengers and I have never heard such a sorry tale please be assured we will never travel with you again."

"Hello Duncan just phoning to wish you a good holiday."

It took him a few seconds to let the penny drop, then we laughed, apparently a friend who was in the house at the time said that Duncan had blown up like a frog when he picked up the phone and shouted "We are first class!"

We had other good friends that lived in Lee Green and Alan a near neighbour had ordered some glass from Lee Green Glass. I rang Jenny his wife, said I was Lee Green Glass and that her husband had ordered a sheet of glass. Jenny knew he had but had no idea of what the size would be. "Well madame your glass is ready can you collect it today?"

"Uh what size is it?" she asked.

"It's eight foot by six feet."

"Oh dear I've only got a Ford Escort."

Other friends had dance lessons offered. Once I was even Victor Sylvester's lead dancer.

Someone up there had also got news on my dissatisfaction because I had a call from Berry, my friend from the Nerja days. He was the godfather of a girl whose father, Berry's friend, was looking for an entrepreneur that was fluent in several languages and could handle salesmen and develop a business idea in the oil industry.

That sounded like me except I could only utter about three words in Spanish, five in German and a few in French. Berry arranged a meeting with Walter Drysdale who had set up an organisation in Regent Street named, The Offshore Centre. He wanted to start business development events wherever oil was being found and produced. And would I go to Regent Street in the West End and meet him. You bet. I telephoned him and we agreed to meet in the Army and Navy Club, on Pall Mall.

I met him there, he was a retired army officer, and much more relaxed than I had expected. He told me what his plans were. He had an idea to start a type of business club for the oil industry – maybe having conferences in the UK and business missions to oil producing countries. He was at present arranging his first conference on Oil Development in the Middle East, at the Hyde Park Hotel and had some fifty odd delegates already registered. He wanted someone with drive, used to handling people, used to sales and could pass in some languages.

CHAPTER 21

I gave him a glowing report on my activities, business development in Spain, International sales, building up sales forces and generally that I had a chequered career, could mix in any society, used to persuading people to see the sense in my ideas, and like him I knew the oil industry was the next growth sector. We drank a couple of bottles of wine, he told me he had been in the army and lost most of his innards in the war, but he could still sink a few drams of malt and that he thought we could get on together. What did I want from him?

I asked about the business club, how did he see that working? He thought he could get companies to pay an annual fee and the Offshore Centre would provide opportunities at conferences and missions abroad to generate business. I suggested that would work if he could attract the right companies to get it started, but what about creating a club atmosphere in your offices, how big were they?

He said "Let's get a taxi and have a look at them."

In the taxi he offered me a job as general manager of the centre, he had backing and he had three floors in an office block opposite Liberty's in Regent Street.

The offices were quite spacious, he had a secretary and Graham his business partner. He introduced me to them as 'our new general manager'. On the second floor, there were three other offices with unmanned desks. The third floor was totally empty, quite large, had a little bar, a sink, and an empty fridge behind the bar. "This could easily be a club room," I commented. "It's big enough to hold meetings for at least thirty people.

The company was named 'The Offshore Centre", and what better place for such an organisation than Regent Street. A bit of a distance from being offshore. But the idea was to develop a membership of mainly service and supply companies and generate business for them. What ideas did I have? At that time some of the operators – BP, Shell, Texaco, Chevron, Marathon Oil etc. were beginning to find oil, or so I had read in doing a bit of research before I met him. I thought if we could persuade them to give presentations to the industry on development plans and what support and equipment they would need, we would have a market and something of real value for our potential members.

We spent some time going through my role and what he wanted and agreed that I would start in two weeks time on the Monday. The Middle East conference would be about three weeks after that giving me time to get associated with the requirements of a conference. The basis of the conference was the role of Saudi Arabia in the developing oil industry. I couldn't even say Saudi as my Norfolk upbringing had always given me problems with pronunciation of words with 'a's and 'u's. So I spent the two weeks practising with some tutorage from Mary on how to say Saudi.

I thanked Berry for his introduction and we played golf again at Roehampton during my two weeks wait. He was a stickler for correct dress and I had arrived in another somewhat tatty sweater, He said you can't wear that in the clubroom Brian, I want to buy you a new one. I demurred and was fitted out, my old sweater found its way into my boot, I can use that for gardening I told him. We had a couple of games during the two weeks and he talked about Nerja and his narrow escape from losing his money. He also complained bitterly about the Labour governments restrictions on overseas holiday allowances. As I had very little money I couldn't get worked up about it but I agreed with him and each day he bought me a good lunch.

I was excited about starting up in a completely new field to me and on the Friday before my start date I got a call from Sue, Walter's secretary, to say he had had a heart attack and would not be working for some time, I was to look after the conference.

I really knew nothing of the oil industry and the conference was weighing heavily on my mind. I would have to introduce the panel of speakers – all budding experts in the industry. Luckily Walter had arranged for the head buyer of Brown and Root to be chairman for the event. I threw myself on his generosity and asked if he could he take the opening of the conference and would he manage it – he became an instant friend.

I busied myself and got to know Walter's friend and partner, Graham who had also invested in the company and was to be Accounts and Finance Director. Walter's secretary was very helpful, she had only been with the company a few weeks and was also trying to familiarise herself with the oil industry.

I went to meet our chairman for the Saudi conference, Brown & Root were then one of the main contractors to the industry and were in a very impressive office. Terry Welch said he would take over the entire day and I could relax. Walter had lined up some speakers and Terry added others so we were able to produce an interesting and informative day for the industry representatives that were registering for the conference.

I can distinctly remember when I went for my interview as a prospective pilot in the RAF, I had been very nervous and I tried not to let it show. I wish I had known that I was colour blind so I could have missed that anxiety. Not knowing anything about what I was about to do left me a little short on self-confidence. Acting, palm reading, working in Nerja mainly with professional people – many extremely successful had given me a much needed boost. But I suddenly felt a little chill of apprehension. I knew nothing about the oil industry, I had met some people involved in the industry through Keith, but I had learned very little about the actual procedures involved.

Terry said that he and Walter had drawn up a list of speakers that had confirmed their involvement, experts in the Middle East, oil company men and someone from our own government that was involved in oil development in the Middle East. Terry would run the conference and he would do the introduction to it. Its aims, and objectives would be down to him. He would keep the necessary pace and he would handle a question and answer period at the end of the day. He would also introduce me to all the speakers at the start of the day but would not elaborate on my knowledge other than to say I was new to the Offshore Centre and the oil industry.

With Terry's help I invited some of the press to the day – they represented various monthly magazines, plus some of the leading newspapers – we needed publicity. I also helped Walter's secretary with founding a list of companies that were active or wanted to be in the industry and I progressed the idea of having presentations on potential projects. The top floor of our offices was big enough to house presentations for up to 40 people. There was a little kitchen in a small room. I ordered folding chairs and purchased a projector and an overhead projector. We were ready. But I would need a secretary.

The conference went well, Terry was magnificent. I sat in at the back and tried to absorb the information that was given out. I could see that conferences would be very instructive for the delegates providing the selected speakers were really in a position to advise. I guess I would have to try to create my own until Walter returned. I also thought about the club idea and membership. If we arranged regular conferences then members could have entry to these at reduced prices or they could be arranged exclusively for member companies.

I congratulated Terry on his handling of the speakers and the question and answer period at the end. We discussed Walter's idea of a membership scheme. We agreed we would need several programmes to make it attractive to companies, and we would need to keep abreast of the industry which was just showing signs of real activity in the North Sea. He told me which magazines we should have at the Centre, keep an eye on projects and read all I could to get myself into the industry.

I talked to some of the press and told them our plans, and we got some publicity. My next object was to mail the companies we had earmarked as potential members and we offered membership to all the major oil companies, some of them took us up which helped with getting service companies interested.

I discussed with Graham, the financial partner in the centre what I thought would be the best way to get companies into the idea of a members club. Perhaps we could put on small discussion groups at the centre on the top floor. Get leading figures in oil companies to give talks on projects they hoped to develop. Graham asked why they would want to do that? I thought, I guess communication is the thing. If the industry is going to take off in this country it will be just as important that the service industry is on a par with operators so they can work together. He agreed. I suggested I would see if Sue and I could get books that listed companies that are already involved with the industry and approach them initially to get information.

We mailed all the main oil companies – most of whom were situated in the greater London area, suggesting that the oil industry needed a business centre that could look at real communication between all sectors. Our plan was to develop relations and exchange knowledge that could be shared and the operators would benefit from openness. It was successful and, led by BP, some of the majors joined the centre. We then promoted the idea to the main contractors stating that we now had some of the operators as members and it would be essential for them to be alongside these. Lastly we mailed the service industry proposing that they could use the centre as a meeting place and could attend presentations by the operators at which they could discuss their development plans and their requirements.

Walter was making good progress in his health and now appeared for a few hours each week. We went to one of the first major oil related exhibitions at Earls Court and left promotional material on the centre at all the exhibiting companies. On the way back to our office I said what if we turned that around and produced a meeting where the companies that exhibit were to come to meet their clients, purchasing people, specifying engineers and the like from oil companies. Call it a workshop and guarantee all delegates at least six appointments during the day. We could get a major oil company that was about to develop a project to allocate some of their project people, their engineers and purchasing people to attend. We could give 20 minute talks – meetings for all the delegates, blow a whistle or ring a bell to indicate change and co-ordinate all the meetings. It would also help the major oil companies to appreciate and meet with a wide variety of reliable service companies in one day.

We listed the projects that were in various stages of development, the oil companies that had found oilfields and my target was to get them to agree to workshops meeting up with most of the service companies that were already accepted in the industry, many of them members of the centre. The great hall in the Grosvenor House Hotel on Park Lane was our room, it was ideal for the hordes of companies that wanted to be involved and it trebled our membership.

We then set up a regular promotion for Oil companies to give presentations and then would follow up with workshops for service companies to introduce their products/services to the majors. Within a short time the centre was booming. Walter suddenly wanted to change the name and call it the Energy Business Centre, he wanted to include other forms of energy, we added to our staff and promoted the idea and we also introduced the idea of overseas missions to oil producing countries.

We had a good cross section of companies as members. We then bought a 16 mm projector as ETPM one of Frances major contractors and pipe layers wanted one for their presentation, it would be on the 'Straits of Magellan" – how pipe would be laid and what was required. This was of interest to the oil companies and also the service industry. I arranged that we should also have a lunch and gave *Uncommon Cooks* their first job. The lady that was setting up the company was a personal friend in

Blackheath and she had told me she wanted to launch a catering company. Our first presentation was a success, forty members attended. The presentation was in the morning and then we had a question and answer period followed by lunch and a chance to meet and mingle.

We had several presentations and as the attending numbers outgrew the centre we started using the Connaught rooms – quite close to the centre. The pattern of oil companies giving a presentation on their next project became very popular, oil was being discovered in the North Sea and gas off East Anglia and the Midlands and the industry became massive. Aberdeen was growing at an alarming rate and most of the operators opened offices there.

I started arranging Maintenance conferences in Aberdeen, the first one was in the Old Skean Du hotel on the airport, it was in September and the hotel had a swimming pool, two of us ventured in and it was the coldest water I have ever been in. But it did focus my mind on why I was there and whilst it was early days to be involved in maintenance we had several conferences – all very well attended – and it gave me a good overview of Aberdeen. I would go up anyway for the Offshore Exhibition every other year where just about every company with an interest in oil exhibited in some capacity.

Mexico was rapidly becoming a target for the industry and I went there to try to set up a programme bringing in their oil related companies to a conference for two days followed by workshops for the European companies we would approach to try to get involved. I was very impressed with Mexico City and having arrived and booked into my *My Isobella Maria Hotel* I travelled in an open taxi to Pemex, the National Oil Company. By open, I mean the Volkswagen had no doors and the driver was a kamikaze man. I was treated royally, by the Promotions and Engineering directors and eventually met the president of Pemex. He listened to my suggestions and then suggested that he could get the President of Mexico to give the welcome and opening speech for the conference. He thought this would be very possible as Mexico was definitely looking to expand their industry and would welcome European involvement. This was big time. I had told Pemex that we would be assured of many European oil companies and the main contractors to the industry would be involved, keeping my fingers crossed.

When I finished my meeting their promotions director offered to show me some of the ancient sights near Mexico City the following day. I particularly liked Garibaldi Square where thirteen mariachi bands were marching round the perimeter. We looked at a place he called Heaven on Earth which was the remains of the huge lake that Mexico City had been built on. There were countless small canals on which were the touring boats and punts, little boats carrying carpets, photographers, barbecues and a myriad of services all to satisfy the tourists in their tours of the waterways. When I left Pemex I was told a car would take me to my hotel but immediately outside the main entrance was a fairly big tin hut which was built like an upside down half round space ship, in it was a couple of men who were offering freshly squeezed oranges, something I had never had in my life, so I had a glass of it and it was superb. I was tickled by the fact that this very ramshackle building was right in front of the main entrance to the major oil company of Mexico

I telephoned Walter and said what success it had been and for him to start preparing a brochure with the European conference speakers listed headed by the President of Mexico. I returned first class with B Cal and we went through the most horrific storm I had ever seen. The plane dived and dropped, waved its wings and we all pulled out safety belts tighter.

On returning to the Centre we were informed that yes the President of Mexico would open the conference. I was then very busy promoting Mexico to the European oil industry and we eventually had fifty three delegates representing the cream of the industry. I hired a promotions company from Edinburgh to create a slide show covering all our companies, what they did, and their achievements in oil development. They would produce the show with some eight projectors using slides from each company and giving every indication of a moving film and they would accompany us to Mexico.

Walter's secretary arranged all the flights which was actually quite complicated as some were from the UK, others from Holland, Norway, France and we had the cream of the burgeoning oil industry, we were all to stay in the *Hotel My Isobella Maria*, where I had first stayed. I went out in advance to tie in with Pemex all the necessary background of support and our delegates started arriving.

Bill Landale headed the Edinburgh film company, he travelled with an enormous amount of equipment which took some time to get cleared by customs, and a few notes had to be handed over to acquire it. In the middle of our week there his father died and he became a Laird inheriting some thousands of acres of land south of Edinburgh.

Walter and his wife arrived and I quickly gave him a tour of the city and took him to Pemex where we checked everything was in order for the conference to start on the Monday morning. On the Sunday we all went to the Heaven on Earth centre and I foolishly ate a very hot dish from one of the open grills near the entrance. We had great fun in several punts being rowed and pushed through the waterways, but later that evening I retired early as I didn't feel very well and that night was probably the most upset and painful night of my life. I had Montezuma's revenge and was up most of the night. Somehow I dragged myself to the conference the next morning but Walter told me to go back to the hotel and stay in bed – he would look after the conference. I spent the whole day being very sick and a local doctor gave me some horse pills and instructed me to just drink water all day.

That night some of the delegates came to see me and I eventually perked up a bit but it was not until the next lunch time that I had something to eat. I suffered for several weeks before I eventually felt better. On the third night some of us were sitting in a bar, I was drinking neat whisky as one of the older delegates had said it was the best medicine for ailing stomachs, and across the table from me was one of our delegates who was entertaining us when I noticed a stags head behind him on the wall nodding. I thought this whisky is powerful but some other things also started to move and then a scream went up – Earthquake! We all rushed out into the street and for about two minutes there was a deep rumbling all around us, it was quite frightening, but it passed and we eventually settled back. The whole conference and workshop was a great success and several of the European companies were invited to set up joint ventures and help Mexico with its development.

My next project was to lead and promote a group of European companies to Canada where oil had been discovered offshore in Newfoundland. Again I went over in advance to set up a programme, first to Newfoundland, then Halifax, then on to Calgary which was already the centre of Canada's oil industry.

Newfoundland was like stepping back into the 1930's. Union flags were very much in evidence and I learnt a few tricks of the local trade. I was introduced to Screech, apparently they would export fish in barrels to Jamaica and the barrels would be returned full of rum, you took a swig of rum and screeched. The other tall story was that as an iceberg floated past you could knock off a bit and put it into your gin and tonic.

The amusing thing was that Newfoundland would often be covered in mist and fog when icebergs were close, so they, being aware of the sudden interest in the area because of the offshore discovery, decided to build a runway in the least affected area which happened to be in the middle of a forest near the centre of the island. They cleared all the trees and the airport was built but, as soon as the foggy conditions appeared it would plonk itself down on the large cleared runway site. I eventually had a group of 23 oil people and we landed on a clear day and spent two days in meetings and a conference. When it came to flying out to start a two day meeting in Halifax the fog was so dense we were grounded. I eventually found a one man airline that would take us to Halifax but it would be circuitous landing at several little airports trying to avoid the fog. I had the most memorable breakfast served by a very tall air hostess, the only one on the aircraft, of bacon, fried bread, little sausages and maple syrup. How she managed to provide this to all 24 of us no one knew, but it was superb. We had lost half a day in Halifax and as we had the Prime Minister of Nova Scotia giving the welcome speech everyone – both Canadian and our delegates – knuckled down to work very much longer and later than planned. Halifax was in its infancy in oil terms but some of our companies were offered business opportunities there.

We then went on to Calgary, what a town! The Stampede was on, everyone was dressed in jeans and many wore large cowboy hats and high heeled boots. There were chuck wagons in the streets serving bacon and breakfasts. On the first night I immediately arranged for tickets to see it, cowboys riding bucking broncos, snorting bulls – we loved it. The *Four Seasons* hotel was also a hit with the group, the weather was very warm, the pool was a definite attraction and we somehow managed to fit in several workshops and presentations.

Once back to London I started to arrange presentations and workshops with the oil majors who had projects to develop and the centre went from strength to strength. We were prospering, but somehow my relationship with Walter deteriorated and when he gave me a dairy as a Christmas present I initially couldn't believe it as I/we had provided sufficient money for him to buy a new house. So I did the sensible thing and set up my own company in direct opposition, taking with me Carolyn as a partner and Judy my secretary. I was offered an office in Great Windmill Street in Soho by my friend, Jack Stein and we were immediately offered a joint venture with an American company, ICE, International Conferences and Exhibitions in China. We were to promote the show with obvious interest in the oil industry and the first exhibition was POWER in Beijing.

CHAPTER 22

Visit to China 1980
Dear Mr Ling, Mr Ding, Mr Li, Mr Lu.

When I knew for certain (my ticket to travel had arrived) that I was going to China, my apprehension grew. I started to gather information from seasoned travellers (2 visits) to passers through (1 visit) about China, These were not easy to find. China remained veiled in mystery and secrecy. China was a long way away from Soho where my office was, even though the Chinese quarter was part of that sector of London and I was a regular visitor to have some tasty dim sum.

We understood Japan, after all, every second car is Japanese, Cherry's, Sunny's, Nissans. Buyers of steel are inundated with Japanese suppliers.

China, well China was out there somewhere, she was growing at an alarming rate, and she was showing signs of opening her doors, raising the bamboo curtain. Major organisations were bending over backwards to be seen to be amenable and providing for the trade delegations or engineers on a learning curve who were visiting our shores. But for me China remained a mystery.

I gathered stories – you'll find its freezing in Beijing this time of year, November/ December, take thermal underwear, take a wool cap, your brains will freeze. My brains will freeze? Well what few I have were not happy about this, should I really be going? I drew comfort from the fact that I knew people did go and their brains remained intact.

One story frightened me. "You'll find rats and cockroaches in your hotel rooms."

"Are you sure"? I asked, turning a pale shade of grey.

"Sure, my director in one country town sat up in his bed all night petrified as the rats sniffed round his room and cockroaches rained down from the ceiling, he was in shock for a month after his return."

"There are very few cars in China, they all cycle, you'll no doubt ride around in a cycle taxi."

"Buses," I said, "are there any buses?"

"No buses for visitors or taxis."

"Won't it be very cold and slow riding around on a bicycle?"

Ah drinks. "The Chinese are great drinkers?"

"No, not really. You'll probably be able to get beer but I doubt if you will find wine, I think they have a spirit that's often used for paint stripping."

The language, I thought I had better learn the language. I knew my partner Carolyn, was not looking forward to going to China. Now, the Far East was her patch. She was born in Australia. I wondered how the Chinese would view a woman. Anyway she had led missions to countries near China, she had property out there somewhere. She knew the way of life, why should she be scared? This was really getting through to me.

On Sunday in church I was impressed by the sermon, every time I went to church at that time I heard a sermon that pulled at my conscience. They weren't about China as such but they were often about Christians in other countries with totally different cultures. I talked to the Vicar at the end of one service and he said he would find me a book on Christianity in China. It arrived the day I was leaving and I put it into my case to read on the plane.

Qing, please. *Xei Xei* thank you. *Nee How* hullo. *Zi Jian* goodbye. I hoped they were impressed with the fact I was at least trying to learn their language. I worried about my pronunciation. Was it correct? Would I be telling them to get stuffed because I made the wrong sound, if so would they throw me into jail because of my rudeness. Ah well, I thought, cold, cockroaches, rats, solitude, not asking for muesli for breakfast. Maybe I can catch flu or Chinese measles on the day before I have to go.

Injections – You'll need injections. But I don't like injections, I hate injections. You should have injections, you need malaria pills, you need polio inoculation, you need typhoid, you need cholera, possibly yellow fever. I was quaking with fear, maybe if I put it off until the last minute they would give me one large tablet, pat me on the bum and say, no problem ol' chap, this is cure for everything, it preserves life, takes away all your urges, stops reaction, cuts down on the desire to live. Wow, I was rambling, you could positively smell the fear.

My wife Mary said, "You must phone the doctor, arrange a time to have your injections."

"Do I have to?"

"Of course you must, you could get all sorts of dreadful diseases over there."

Another nail of apprehension driven in. "Ok I'll do it today."

She stood over me. "Do it now."

I dialled the doctor, that's it, there was no getting out of it.

I rolled up on my motorbike with my orange oil company jacket flashing its sign. I had my offshore boots on – signs that I was a man of courage – I'd obviously been on a BP platform in the North Sea. The waiting room with its many eyes watched me sit down. I straightened my back and looked casually round the signs on the wall; one picture grabbed my attention, a nurse putting a needle into an arm. I didn't read the words, a hot flush was coming over me. I hastily looked at another picture of hands holding a baby which read, *the first few minutes of life are very precious.* Then underneath someone had written in pen *the last few are pretty important too.* It made me smile. Then with a start I heard, "Mr Banham yellow door please." *God he's even got the colour of the door right, it's a conspiracy,* I thought.

A friendly faced doctor asked me to sit down, "Are you in the oil business?" he asked.

"Oh Yes." I replied.

"What can we do for you?" he smiled.

"I'm going to China soon and I just thought I would enquire if it's necessary to have any sort of injections. I believe that nowadays the Chinese are so advanced it's not, isn't that correct?"

Please Mr Doctor, say that's correct, don't make me –

"Oh No Mr Banham, things can be very rough out there medically you know. You need"

I don't hear what I need, I have withdrawn into a shell of fear, I am getting hot and cold at the same time, my brain is reeling.

He's still talking, "Luckily I have a cholera and typhoid service here and I believe a polio vaccine, but you will need another booster for each in a month's time."

Ah, I grasped at straws. "I am leaving in three weeks, do you think I should put the whole thing off until I return?"

"Well no" he said, "It's a little rushed but you can come back just before you leave. I would make it at least three days before you go, because you will feel the effects for a while."

What effects? Oh God

"Will I be ill"? I enquired, trying not to burst into tears and flee his room.

"Well you will have a sore arm, which arm do you want it in by the way," he stood there with a great big hypodermic needle in his hand.

"Oh does it matter?"

"Well best not in the arm you write with."

Oh No I'll be paralysed in my arm.

"By the way you will need two, this is only for cholera."

"Someone told me they are combined" I scream, clutching at another straw.

"No, he says, not any more, can you take your shirt off."

"May I sit down please, I'm not too good at this sort of thing."

"Sure take your time, we'll do the left arm then."

He wiped it, *Oh God he's doing into my big inoculation spot that I had before I was old enough to know about fear.*

I looked the other way, the prick was like a pile driver driving a 50 foot pile into the North Sea's largest platform. I sat in a daze, he did it again – I was passing out.

"Now open your mouth please."

He's not going to inject my tongue is he?

"Open wide, swallow this" he said.

"Shouldn't I have it on sugar, I heard that somewhere."

"No" he said, "that's for children."

Ugh I kept swallowing.

"Are you alright?" he said, as I attempted to struggle back into my clothes.

"No" I muttered, "I am definitely not good at this."

"Sit down then a bit longer," he suggested. "Breathe deeply." He wrote out a prescription, "These are your malaria tablets, take one a week and continue with them for at least a month after you get back."

I fell out of his room and staggered on to my motorbike, somehow riding it to my office. How long I sat alone I do not know. My secretary came in and asked "You Ok?"

"Oh sure just a bit groggy from all my injections." My plastic grin was in place.

The days passed, by now I could remember, *Xie – Xie Shay shay*, thank you. *Zi Jian* goodbye. I had talks with the commercial counsellor for China in his office at the Standard in Blackheath – The Red House. He promised me help and friendship and gave me pots of tea on each visit.

I was still collecting names of organisations in China that could be of assistance to my exhibitors and I was involved and organising the exhibition in China, Peking (Beijing). Our company, with I.C.E., helped promote the event through the Energy Industries Council. Everyone visiting China had to have an entry visa and this could be quite difficult to obtain. An exhibition was one way of entering. There you see, was a mystery again; they analysed what your company did and if it traded with Taiwan the chances of getting into China were remote, unless of course you had two passports. But that was only for the smart asses who knew the ropes.

I had to visit the doctor again for my follow up booster, I went through my routine of deep breathing but it was just as bad. I somehow survived and collected my two bottles of cholera and typhoid from the fridge. When I got into his surgery it was a young bearded Locum aged about 13. He read books to see what he had to do to me. He also seemed to be nervous because he dropped the serum onto his desk and it rolled onto the floor.

I plaintively requested he used new needles. "The floor isn't that clean."

He dismissed me and said "You'll only feel a little burning sensation."

I burned both times but, there I was ready…

My bags were packed and I had patted the dog. "Look after them Jim" his tail was down, it had been for three days, ever since I brought the case back from the office stuffed with leaflets and brochures. I hope they wouldn't impound them at customs, we didn't get clearance on their content.

When we met the official carrier for the exhibition materials he had given us a very gloomy picture of how precise the Chinese are regarding promotional material, also the amount each company should provide, because the Chinese authority's commandeer about two thirds of your leaflets for distribution among the countless ministries and corporations and what is most important to customs. Ah, customs now, there's a name to make you turn cold.

I had collected my passport from the mews behind Portland Place, ready stamped with a visa, but I still had to collect a passport visa in Hong Kong. This had been suggested by the Chinese exhibition organisers, CCPIT who had my number there. Approval number 106. CCPIT was the China Council for the Promotion of International Trade and were very strict on what can be done there, and how it's done, by any 'outside' organiser. The tip is to get complete approval from them before you venture into any production of leaflets or information that is in any way promotional.

The idea of collecting another visa in Hong Kong worried me a bit as I envisaged an enormous office and taking hours to track down 106, little me, in one of the busiest places in the world... I also like to have everything organised in advance.

I double-checked my passport, my ticket, there and back, my dollar travellers cheques, most important was to have dollars, the mighty dollar speaks loudly anywhere. I had my inoculation papers, the medicines, lip salve, bath oil, body cream, dry skin relief, shampoo, cold sore lotion, opening and sealing tablets – well you never know – electric shaver, I hoped they had an electric supply.

"Got your long john's dad?" The girls had come in to my room to help. "What about thermal underwear? Got your hat?"

"No, I'll buy one there, always fancied a Cossack hat."

"It's China you're going too, not Russia." said Jess.

Reading books, warm clothes, shut the case, I'm ready.

My wife had the car running, it was still light and we all climbed in – all except Jim the dog. He looked distinctly sad and had been limping on three legs all yesterday. I wondered, dogs have a sixth sense, maybe he was trying to tell me something.

We swept off to Gatwick, Mary asked me to drive as she will have to on the way back. We talked about anything other than what we were doing. The motorway said Gatwick and then we arrived. We all hugged and kissed; Frankie our oldest gave me a really comforting hug, then Jess and then Mary. We held each other close and she smiled comfortingly at me then climbed back into the car and I waved to them as they drive away.

I hoped I'd remembered everything, patting my pockets as I arrive at check in. I am flying B Cal. I loved British Caledonian. I had for some time given the airline free space at all my exhibitions and meetings in the oil industry, in return I had a contra deal to fly either business class, or if they had plenty of space – first...

My bag weighed a ton with all the leaflets. I was hoping they wouldn't charge me excess. I fixed the girl behind the counter hoping she wouldn't notice the weight. "Very full tonight? no smoking please, as far forward as possible please."

She smiled and spent a great deal of time on her terminal. Am I on? I began to worry, had the heavy bag broken the system?

"How would 12b do sir? No window seat left I'm afraid."

"Is it an aisle?" I asked.

"Oh yes, of course."

The bag, yes I only have one bag and this hand luggage. I tried to make it look like a child's toy, doing my strongman act, standing on one foot – it's also stuffed with leaflets.

"Fine" she said, "you will be called at 9.20."

I headed for the 'Clansman lounge.' Now the Clansman lounge is another thing; B Cal said you have a choice and I believed it. I staggered in under the weight of my hand luggage and booked in. The telly was on, a glass of champagne arrived – I'm travelling.

I enjoyed my time in the Clansman, I was mollycoddled. I think my friend at B Cal had asked them to see that I was 'taken care of'. I was escorted to the check-in and seen through to my seat, which was next to a rotund gentlemen – he was a civil engineer that didn't play crib or backgammon. We had some sixteen hours to pass. I had done plenty of flying over the last years yet I always got an excited feeling when first setting out and this time was no exception. I was offered any drink as soon as we were airborne.

My 'fat belly' engineer wanted to talk about the tube train in Hong Kong; he had been involved with its design and building, yes I would be impressed as it had rubber wheels unlike the noisy London tube, yes I should certainly travel on it. I retired into my shell and mumbled a few "of course, yes I would" then a most marvellous meal was served and washed down with champagne. I was ready to sleep. I awoke to see the most magnificent dawn over the Gulf. The sky gradually started to lighten, the grey melted into a fiery orange and quite suddenly the sun appeared, a brilliant orange red ball. It was staggeringly beautiful.

We landed in Dubai and I was fascinated to see there were puddles of water in the sand. It was early morning but the temperature was already in the 70's. The engineer said, "Take your valuables with you, the cleaners can be light fingered". I made my way into the duty free zone and discovered just how much tax goes on a bottle of scotch in the UK. I was fascinated by the trading outpost which, presumably opened its doors every time an aircraft landed, all the shops were staffed by very sleepy looking individuals. Just about anything that one would see in the UK was on show. I studied the cameras, watches, radios, clothes and compared prices, one of my favourite pastimes. Then settled on a bottle of Malt Whisky and a bottle of Ricard.

We all trooped back on to the aircraft, more food – considering how much exercise one gets on a long flight a tremendous amount of food is consumed.

As we approached Hong Kong fat belly stirred himself and said "This must be the most dangerous landing in the world."

"Why" I said looking round for a pretty air hostess to hold hands with.

"Well the aircraft has to fly between tower blocks aiming at a mountain then at the last minute bank sharply to the right and land."

"Wow, you've done this many times?" I asked between grated my teeth.

"Yes" he says, "the runway is built out into the sea and these B Cal pilots seem to put it down very late."

I needed more than a hand to hold. I tightened my strap, as we started flying between blocks of flats, lights were beginning to appear everywhere, the aircrafts wings seemed to be brushing the tv aerials on the flats.

"How much further to the mountain," I casually asked.

"Oh any minute now," he said. With that the plane suddenly swooped down to the right, straightened out and the ground was rushing past.

"Put it down," I muttered through clenched teeth.

We bump, then again and we are down, reverse thrust goes on at a high pitched roar and the aircraft slows down to a manageable speed.

"That wasn't too bad." I smiled casually at old fat belly.

Hong Kong airport must be the most efficient place to pass through in the world, there are dozens of customs clerks. I was stamped and through in a matter of seconds collected my bag and pushed my trolley past the customs checkpoint. I was waved over to the counter. "Where you flom" the clerk asked.

"England." I replied.

"Any contraband, any firearms?"

"You're joking," I smiled back. He waved me through.

When you step out of the huge concrete square tunnel at Hong Kong airport you step out into an incredible world. I see the sign Hotel cars, there is so much noise, fast moving cars, buses, taxis, hotel cars, mini buses, and the odd Rolls Royce, all careering about, seemingly bent on destruction with each other as there are squeals of brakes and voices shouting all the time.

Along the road are hotel signs A – Z mounted about 15 feet high. I went to the M's *Mandarin*. A white Mercedes pulled up. "You for Mandarin?"

"Yes."

Out leapt a young man and he grabbed my cases pushed them into the boot and he held open the door for me – all seemingly within the same moment. Is it free, I think, I found out later that it isn't but it was very impressive.

I climbed in and he jumped into the driving seat and off we went. "My name Sammy Chen" said my driver. "What your name?"

Well, what the hell I think, "*Ugh* Banham – Brian Banham."

"OK Banham," he said "You here on horriday?"

"No just a couple of days on my way to China."

"China ey," he said tipping his hat over his eyes. "You call, me Sammy, you terrryphone Sammy when you want lide Hong Kong."

He chats away, eventually I ask him where he learnt his English. "I rearn my Engrish flom visitors rike you."

We were funnelling into the new tunnel linking Kowloon with Hong Kong island, the traffic if anything is even more crowded and moving very fast, we eventually emerged at the other end, he increased speed again and suddenly a van pulled out directly in front of us. He blasted on his horn as he braked and shouted "sirry Frucker". He smiled in the mirror at me. "Rots of sirry fruckers driving vans" he said.

We pulled up at the Hotel. Several flunkies were standing around the main entrance, they quickly surrounded the car. I was whisked away to reception, a small grey haired man stepped out from the Chinese faces, "Mr Banham, please come this way."

"What about my cases?" I asked

"Don't worry they will come."

He led me into the most sumptuous suite with a huge bunch of flowers on the central table. He gave me a registration form to fill in. I wondered whether everyone got this treatment. Then he said we will meet later to discuss your group. Group ... then it dawns on me, some weeks ago when booking the hotel I had said that I was going into China to set up an exhibition and I would eventually be bringing many delegates and exhibition staff. And we would no doubt be staying over in Hong Kong to get used to the time change. Umm, better use that approach wherever I go I thought.

I looked round the suite, a magnificent bathroom with two bath robes. Dozens of little packets and boxes of goodies, wonderful view out over the harbour. I started to make myself at home by dropping clothes around the immaculate main room, the doorbell rang and a flunkie was there with an enormous cornucopia of fruit; every imaginable fruit was there, including some I have not seen before.

I decide to go to the top floor where there is a swimming pool, I dressed in one of my bathrobes and shuffle off. The pool it was not very big and only one person was swimming but there was an attendant at each end of the pool. I slipped out of my robe and one of the attendants came over to me and asked if he could look after it for me. I slipped in, it was not too deep. I am not the best swimmer in the world and I only did one length and pulled myself up to sit on the edge at the other end. The other attendant stepped forward with a towel, "No not yet" I said. The other swimmer, a Japanese man, swam up to me, pulled himself onto the ledge and introduced himself. He asked what I did, and as I replied he pulled out of his swimming trunks a plastic card, with his name and company on it. I was amazed, and thanked him and swam three lengths of the small pool then decided that's it. The attendant wanted to dry me at least that was what I thought ...No thanks.

I got back to my suite and decided to go to the main sitting room in the hotel before having my dinner. There was the most beautiful Chinese lady playing the piano, she was singing Moon Libber. I sat there entranced and highly amused. With my first drink I was given a book on the hotel. It has just been voted the second best hotel in the world. I wondered if they have found the first yet?

After a wonderful dinner I decided to do the peak. I travelled up a perilous hillside railway track. Fairyland, lights everywhere, the view of the harbour was magic. I looked at the display board which described what all the buildings were and watched the Star Ferry come chugging over from Kowloon, making a note that to take the ferry myself the next day. I was beginning to feel the long journey and decided to go back to bed. That night I slept in the biggest bed I had ever seen.

Next day at breakfast, Carolyn my business partner has arrived, she was only in a junior suite and was a bit envious of my fruit and flower story. We both decided to go to Nathan Road, apparently, so we had been told, you could buy anything on Nathan Road. I had a cashmere jacket made which would be delivered to my hotel later that day. What service! What about a fitting? It will be ok, the salesman assured me. If not when I came back from China he would refit it.

The time arrived to prepare for China, I packed my fruit and Hong Kong bargains. Carolyn had to get to Beijing via Canton for some reason. C.A.A.C. Caac by name caac by nature someone said. C.A.A.C. China Airways Administration Corporation had routed her via Canton even though she had made her booking three weeks before I did. My jacket arrived, and it fitted perfectly.

The Mercedes was waiting – you do pay for it but its all done so efficiently that there is no chore attached to travelling. We were met at the airport by the hotel assistant, our bags were whisked through to CAAC. Carolyn went to the Canton desk with the assistant to see if she could get a re-routing with me direct. No one held out any hope of this and as I waited patiently in my queue I saw her disappear.

My bags were even heavier. I had discovered that B Cal doesn't charge for extra weight, but did CAAC? The weighing terminal raced around the clock as I heaved my main bag on to it.

"Is that your only luggage?"

"No, I have this little hand luggage," doing my casual light load bit. I left my bag of fruit on the floor so he couldn't see it.

"OK. Will you wear this sticker" he said, "It's for China, all people going to China wear these." He stuck an enormous red C on my chest and pointed the way to my departure gate and I slid away clutching my passport, fruit, and boarding card.

Why should I get a sticker, no one else has a sticker, what's so different about me; could it be the heavy case? The old worries start to impinge, I wandered up to a photographic shop as I had a little time to kill and eventually found a zoom lens going for a song, well a meagre sum. I brought a couple of films and wondered about buying more but I guessed they have films in China.

Time arrived for me to go to my 'disembarkation' point. I pushed my trolley with the very heavy hand luggage and my bag of fruit up to the entrance, four young girls appeared from behind a wall and one noticed my C, "You can't go through here. You must go further on prease."

I pushed past three more entrances until I was waved into a small cubicle by a very muscular looking lady in uniform.

"Leave your trolley out there" she commands, I heaved my heavy bag onto the counter, my fruit bag was in my hand. She peered at it "You have flute in there?"

I am amazed, how did she know? "Yes, why?" I said

"Not allowed take flute into China."

"What shall I do with it" I enquire meekly.

"You must eat" she says looking frosty. She let me through and came with me to where there were some seats and I got out a furry fruit and an apple. I started to eat the apple and realised there is no way I could eat all this fruit. I looked over towards a sign and peering at me from the side of the sign were three little Chinese faces grinning at me. I asked them if they would like my fruit and they pointed to another counter where a man in uniform was watching me. I went over and asked him if the three children and his staff would like some fruit.

"Flute" he said "yes prease." He looked into the bag, "velly good flute you should eat."

"No thanks me have prenty" I meant plenty but he didn't notice. I waved at the three kids and pointed to my bag and calmly walked off towards my gate heaving my heavy bag.

It was gate 24. Why is it always the furthest point when you have a heavy load? I noticed a few more people with a big C on their chests... *Phew that's OK then...*

I went to the designated number and sat under a rumbling air condition unit, put my bag on the floor and started reading my book on 'what to expect in China. I noticed I was becoming surrounded by a very colourful crowd of French speaking people, some were pulling their hand luggage in neat little four wheel jobs, others had hardly anything except a packet of Gauloises and a lighter. Actors, they must be actors, well things were looking up. French actors in China.

Our flight number was called, we all trooped through the check gate and eventually walked out onto the tarmac and then up towards our aircraft. It was a Russian built Illysian – it gave the impression that we would be flying in a long propelling pencil and the engines looked like eyelashes on the wings. I found myself sitting next to an Irish doctor and his wife. They were on a tourist visa and staying in the same hotel as me, Jingoua. We waited for drinks to be brought round, and we waited, not a sign of any hostess for about twenty five minutes. When they did appear they were wheeling a trolley and they slapped out a bowl filled with rice and some brown looking meat on it, there was also an apple for everyone. A glass of water was offered, and tea would come later… Umm B Cal could learn something here!!!

I chatted with the doctor about what to expect in China and what I was doing, he seemed very relaxed about his trip and said that he would be in the hands of a guide, so felt he didn't have to make any provisions for language etc. Yes he would see the Great Wall, the Ming Tombs, the Forbidden City, he had it all planned.

Suddenly going in to land, the ground flashed past us, miles of flat landscape sped past the wing tips, we noticed a few rather dilapidated aircraft standing in bays.

We eventually rolled up to the main building and after some minutes were told to get off. The French group were all sitting up front and as the curtains were pulled back we could see the tiniest first class. We walked down the steps onto the tarmac and had to pass four young soldiers all armed with rifles. We were shown the way to some steps which led up to what is normally swung out and fixed to the entrance or exit of aircraft, climbed these and emerged into a long hall with a moving staircase up the middle. Being naturally lazy and laden with my heavy hand luggage, I like most of the others stepped on to the moving walk-way. and we slowly trundled up towards a raised platform, the walkway stopped, a few of the presumably wise ones walking made the odd comment as they overtook us, then it started again, but, in the wrong direction, this caused a great deal of merriment. It shuddered to a stop again and then went forward and we limped up to the main entrance steps where a 'soldier' in uniform, and with a gun, was taking photographs of us all as we entered the check point.

I wonder why he's doing that I thought, am I entering a book of visitors!! I eventually found two queues and joined one of them, it got longer and longer and didn't appear to be moving at all, suddenly everyone peeled off and hurried to a Chinaman and woman that were waving coloured sticks at us – this turned out to be a false alarm.

We moved from queue to queue, gradually getting nearer a checking desk surrounded by Chinese. I eventually got to it and plonked my case down on the desk.

"What you have in there?"

"Oh my personal belongings and a few leaflets for an exhibition I am at."

They went through the bag, nothing incriminating, "OK Now you correct your case."

"I'm sorry what did you say." I had temporarily forgotten the l's and r's were mixed for them.

"You correct your big case!" He said

"OK, Thanks where is it?"

"It will be in the hall through that door with all the others then you check your case through customs OK?"

"Thank you" I muttered. How long will this take I thought. I had already been in China for nearly an hour and a half and had only got through the first check.

I went through the door to chaos, bags were strewn all over the large room and at the far end was a shelf with rollers on it that had a case with a very bright light behind it and a wide-eyed staring Chinaman looking at the case. Was this their way of checking a case, the light didn't begin to shine through the case so it was a show… no doubt someone in authority had seen cases being passed through customs elsewhere and this was their answer. I felt sorry for the viewing Chinaman, how long would his eyesight last staring at a powerful light bulb all day.

After some pulling and pushing I found my case, it seemed even heavier. I joined the queue to have my bag screened, as it went through I pulled it off the rollers and went towards an EXIT sign – Wow, engrish I thought at last. There was a door I had to go through and there were at least twenty faces ringed around the door, some must have been kneeling, others standing on top of the kneeling ones, there was hardly an inch of doorway without a face. All were saying, cally your case Mr, and one or two shouting taxi Mr.

I managed to push my way through and look around for a driver with my name on his card. Sure enough there he was nonchalantly standing near a big sign saying *Smoke Guards*...I went over.

"Hurro Mr Banham, my name is Bing, You call me Bing. I am your driver for while you are here as arranged by your secretary." Great I thought it does work.

He loaded my cases in with a grunt and a belch. We set off. The car was an old Russian vehicle built with little curtains in the windows at the rear. The road was wide and there were one or two buses standing in the car park. I was surprised to see these, but he started blowing his horn almost at once and he carried on most of the way. There were hundreds of bicycles everywhere; there were also street sweepers everywhere. It was amazing, there were women sweeping up leaves as they fell from the trees on either side of the road and they had plastic bags over their heads to keep the dust out of their nostrils. People on bicycles also had plastic bags on and they were all dressed in a dark blue uniform. How many of them died through asphyxiation? I wondered. China's policy of keeping everyone working I guess.

The driver started to belch as we drove and the car was filled with the smell of sweet garlic. I tried to open a window but he said "No, its too dusty, keep window shut."

It took forty minutes to get to the hotel. After pouring me out of the car he asked "What time do you want me tomorrow."

"I think about 10am will do." I wondered if Carolyn had arrived yet.

I was quite surprised by the architecture, apparently Swiss designed and built fairly recently, there were only two hotels of any quality in Beijing, The Friendship and the Jiangou.

There was a line of Chinese girls standing at reception, four very ordinary looking and one a real stunner, I aimed at her, "Hurro" she says, with the most beautiful smile "What your name?"

"Brian umm Banham and yours?"

"I am Luby, I book you in."

"Has Mrs Wilden arrived yet?"

She checked. "No not yet."

I had a decent room with a little balcony outside, which after opening the door and trying it I decided I would stay inside. It was even dusty there as we were quite close to the main road leading to Tiananmen Square.

I had a shower, then decided to go down and check out the hotel. It had a small bar and a restaurant. I looked at the menu, yes. Yes I could eat here. I was enjoying my first G&T when I heard Carolyn's strident voice at the reception, demanding a drink. That's the Australian's for you I thought. I went through and greeted her, "Come into the bar, what do you want?"

We exchanged stories, her experiences were on a par with mine. We were both amused by the 'electronic' check for baggage, she had had a driver that knew the ropes and got her to the hotel in 30 minutes.

She checked into her room, and then we had a meal our first meal in China it was pretty basic; none of the sweetmeats we get in England. We discussed our movements the next day, we were to meet the American Lawyer for the exhibitors at the Russian exhibition centre.

Mr Bing arrived on time and we set off for the exhibition centre. It was next door to the Zoo and I had a cursory look over the fence to see if I could spot any animals – there appeared to be a Panda near the railings but it had its back to me so I couldn't see what state it was in. We went into the exhibition centre. Some of the companies were already setting up their stands. The exhibition was named Power Generation so we had a good mix of companies that were in that sector, plus some that I knew from the oil industry in the UK.

We met our American. He was white faced red eyed, which I discovered was because he constantly administered eye drops, and was very tall. I nicknamed him Doctor Death and it was a term that stuck. We discussed what our plans were; to follow up as many of the corporations that were involved in power as we could in our week in Beijing. He had some names that he offered and he had a secretary that he hired on a weekly basis when he was in China. She would be pleased to make appointments for us, which we gratefully accepted.

We ended up having lunch with him in the restaurant alongside the exhibition centre. He insisted that we try the local vodka with caviar imported from Russia. It was absolutely superb, the vodka bit into my system so rapidly my words were soon totally blurred. The three of us managed to quaff a whole bottle of the wonderful vodka. We staggered out with most of the afternoon gone in a haze of good friendship. It was very cold outside but I vaguely remember, coming out feeling a great warmth for the world and an ability to do anything. Luckily Bing was still around and he drove us back to the hotel and I asked him in for a drink.

"Not allowed for me to drink in hotel", he explained. "Chinese not allowed with foreigner".

Some time later we walked or more probably staggered, up our road to the Friendship Store and we both bought Chinese coats for a song. I also bought a Cossack Hat and as we looked at the shelves of erotic spices and roots that seem to be a part of China's background the shop girls giggled at us. Long noses we were!

Our schedule of meetings gave us the next day free and we decided to go to the Great Wall and see the Ming Tombs on the way back. Yes Bing was up to that, he would personally take care of us and see that we had one of the best lunches in China. He would be able to eat with us, show us what to eat!

We did the Great Wall, well we walked perhaps half a mile up it -we were both dressed in all our new gear to negate the biting cold. Carolyn had a good experience when she visited the ladies loo. She had to use a cubicle without a door and she had to face towards the wall, when she straightened up it was to see a ring of Chinese faces looking at her private parts with wonder, she came out doubled up with laughter.

The Great Wall is just that, built ranging over mountains and valleys, it is extremely impressive and one is left wondering how all the materials were delivered to the more difficult terrain, and the craftsmanship utilised to perfect it. How many workers died building it? I wondered.

On the way back we stopped at the Ming Tombs and Bing took us to the Ding-a-ling restaurant, alongside the entrance. It was enormous, I wondered if he really knew food. We had an eight course lunch, every course was magnificent and we finished with snow pear. I had great difficulty in describing snow pear on my return. It was a large round fruit a little bigger than a grapefruit, entirely white, succulent and absolutely delicious eaten with a spoon, which sank into the soft fruit, much like a sorbet. Each spoonful was the most satisfying experience.

The Ming Tombs were very interesting but we both wanted to get back as it would be a long journey and once again we were exposed to some rapid driving and frightening near misses. On the way back I enthused over the potential of China. I was used to writing conference programmes and organising supporting exhibitions and so far my exposure to China excited me. I thought that as the industrial world was beginning to look at China as a huge prospect for new business, and China was getting involved in the search for oil. We could combine all the energy sectors in one major show in Beijing.

It would attract the world's energy companies, It could be a Major International Exhibition and Conference and I would entitle it "Total Energy China" Carolyn also got excited about the idea but could we sell it to I.C.E. our American sponsors for this trip?

Dr Death's secretary had been very successful with our appointments. At 9AM we were to see the director of C.N.O.C. a real plum. CNOC being China National Oil Corporation, and we were to see the deputy director of the Natural Gas Corporation in the same building. We may also see the C.O.O.C. director, China Onshore Oil Corporation at the same time. He was trying to juggle his appointments. What a day! We would never get to this level in the UK, and all in one day. I suppose that as we were associated with the first major energy exhibition in Beijing the Chinese were also interested in what we were bringing to them. Our last appointment was with the coal industry at 2pm. Again she promised someone of high level. Don't be late for any of them she warned.

Bing picked us up early and we arrived at the huge building. We went into the door that Bing said was reception. Standing just inside the door was an elegant man in a light blue suit. He said "Mr Barram?"

"Yes"

"I am Deputy Director C.N.O.C, prease be welcome."

He shook both our hands as I introduced Carolyn. We followed him along miles of corridor and through several doors until we came to a big room with desks and chairs all round it. A thermos flask was on each desk and large cups were placed around it. "You have tea?" he asked, and almost immediately another very well dressed man in a light grey suit appeared, the deputy introduced the Director of the C.N.O.C. and said "I will interpret."

Our introduction was interspersed with laughter and masses of tea. So much so that after a while I had to request a visit. Another man came into the meeting with a basic blue uniform and he sported a lot of hair. He turned out to be the Director of the Coal Corporation. He professed not to speak Engrish. Yet a fourth man arrived dressed more conventionally in dark blue. He welcomed us to China, he was the Deputy Director of the C.O.O.C. China Onshore Oil Corporation. He spoke very good English.

I explained what we were doing with the Power Exhibition and that following our visit we were both very impressed with our reception in China and I had an idea for a Total Energy Exhibition and Conference in Beijing. I suggested that it would include all aspects of energy. I could get speakers for the conference from every major sector worldwide that related to energy, even wind farms and electricity supply. I was sure that we would get a very positive response from many countries to take exhibition space. I could see very good financial returns for China plus the added attraction of joint ventures for many Chinese corporations with established companies. I waited for their response.

They talked Chinese for a few minutes and we were given yet more tea. The CNOC Director said, "We could be interested, but we need much more information on its format and what China would have to provide. If we go ahead with it we would prefer that it is held in Canton, Gaungou." He said their main support for the Oil Industry would be based in Guangou. As oil would be the most important development for energy to China, he wanted it to be presented there.

His next question was who would finance this exhibition. I explained that we were in China as representatives of an American exhibition company that had recently opened their main office in the UK and would be operating from London. The Power Exhibition that opens tomorrow is promoted by them and us with support from the Energy Industries Council and the UK government. At the present time the lawyer who represents the American company is in Beijing for the exhibition, but primarily it will be a UK sponsored exhibition, with interest from many countries that are experienced in energy development.

I was getting carried away with this, but I firmly believed it would work; perhaps I was impressed with the level of meetings we were having, I was certainly impressed by the reception. In most countries I have visited one goes through a series of secretaries before getting to the boss. We had been met at the door by the director and he had been waiting for us!! I nearly felt important…

He replied he understood why we were there. He was aware that we represented the exhibition organisers. He had requested information on us whilst Dr Death's secretary had been making appointments. It was the first power exhibition involving foreign companies. He had not expected our proposal but he had been interested in any future plans that our company had in China, hence his interest in meeting us. He would be visiting the exhibition tomorrow and was involved with the opening ceremony. He wanted time to think about my proposal and he would like me to present a full plan of the event within the next month, when he would then decide with the other corporations when would be the best time to mount it.

We left to much more laughter and a great buzz of achievement. When we got outside we realised we had been in the building nearly three hours. But, we had seen all the main energy corporations in one meeting. And, they seemed interested. Yes, I was on a high for the rest of the day. I was also very impressed with their efficiency.

Bing was there belching in his car. "Where you want to go?"

We looked at each other, the rest of our day was free. Lets go to the exhibition hall, show some support for our companies, have another lunch with a bit of caviar, then I would like to go to the Forbidden City.

The exhibiting companies were well on their way to completion, there had been a problem with power earlier. Power, I thought this is a power show. We went round all the UK companies and said we would be there tomorrow for the opening ceremony and left for lunch. I had my first brush with anything that could be interpreted as aggression. I had gone to the toilet which divides the upmarket and the lower level restaurants, whilst peeing a soldier came in and stood three places up from me, looked at me and spat on the floor behind me I ignored that but quickly washed my hands and got out.

We had another memorable lunch, which cost very little and we staggered out, our faces reddened with the very strong Vodka. I bought a bottle of the Vodka which we had been drinking, thinking, "our English friends will enjoy this when I get back". We looked at each other again, the rest of our day was free. Great, what excitement!

Bing then took us to the most remarkable area – The Forbidden City. Single note music greeted us as we entered the main gate which had an enormous picture of Mao Tse Tung. The colours and design of all the buildings was beautiful, superb squares all beautifully paved led us through staggering buildings some of which we were allowed to enter. Lions and gargoyles of various design were guarding many of the entrances. The music, very slow and sedate, occasionally emitting very high notes of singing, bathed us in splendour. It was the most rewarding visit and it took up several hours. Suddenly it was dark and getting very cold. We walked back down the main road to our hotel, both dazzled by what we had seen. I laid in my bath with hot water up to my neck and marvelled at my experiences to date.

The next morning the faithful Bing was outside the hotel, "You have big ceremony?" he asked.

"Not sure what form it will take but we are there representing the organisers"

"Are you speaking?"

"No I think Dr Death is as he speaks a bit of Chinese, and also the UK Government man is replying to the main speech we think."

The CNOC Director was standing in the middle of a great row of Chinese people all dressed in dark blue apart from the director and couple more. There were probably 40 men and one woman in a long line, right across the front of the exhibition hall and there was one microphone in the centre of the line. Dr Death was beside the Director.

For the next hour or so we stood with hundreds of Chinese who have been brought to the hall in the back of army lorries, they were packed in tightly, all standing up in their suits. Speeches rambled on, Dr Death made a speech, some of it translated, some delivered in Chinese. The UK man also gave a warm thank you to the Chinese corporations supporting the exhibition. It was cold, it was tedious but there was no way we could slip off.

The main body of Chinese then visited the exhibition they all grabbed as many brochures as they could lay there hands on. It was remarkable. Some of them had several plastic bags stuffed with brochures. Most of the exhibitors had to ration them out after a while so as to have some for the following days.

That evening we were all invited to a magnificent banquet in the Majestic Peoples Hall in Tiananmen Square, (later famous for when Mrs Thatcher was offered a chickens head during her meal there.).

Eighteen courses were served. On each table was a bowl sitting on a plate, a pair of chop sticks were laying alongside the bowl resting on a little holder shaped like two lions facing inwards. There were four glasses at each place one very small on the outside, a wine glass, a beer glass and we presumed a water glass.

Carolyn and I were on one table with eight Chinamen – the exhibitors were all separated so that each table had about eight Chinese and two or three exhibitors. A short speech of welcome was delivered by the Chinese Government representative. Then an army of waiters and waitresses descended on us. I had been warned by Bing about a required response to any toasting and Gambai would be the toast, which meant bottoms up, empty the glass in one go… A strange smell lingered around the table as the little glasses were filled by the waiters. A Chinaman, obviously the leader of our table picked up his glass and looking at us all raised his and said, Gambai, I lifted my glass to my lips. So that's the smell!! And downed it in one, just as well, it was incredibly strong! It was *MaoTie*, best paint stripper. I winked across the table to Carolyn. She winked back. Luckily we had Bing, Bing had warned us that toasts would be plentiful, it wasn't often ordinary engineers and the like got the chance to eat and drink on the house as it were. So they will keep you at it. BUT... he said, the Chinese were not good at drinking beer so respond with beer toasts. Several bottles of local beer had been placed on the table and also a couple of bottles of deep red wine. I helped myself to a beer and raised my glass to the table and said Gambai. The glass was probably a little under a half pint I put it down in one, even though it took some effort. Our Chinese friends all took their time to consume their beers but they did. That seemed to do the trick.

Some of the most wonderful food was arriving. One course stood out. A beautiful waitress brought a whole suckling pig to our table, it had little lights shining from its eyes – the crackling looked wonderful. She carved off a little square of crackling for each person on the table and the lovely white meat was taken away. It will come again we were assured by the interpreter on our table. The crackling was superb, it melted in the mouth, I needed more beer, I did the same trick with the Gambai and some of the Chinese kept up with us most of them smiling in appreciation. They took on a healthy, glow, and were enjoying themselves.

We staggered through all eighteen courses, most of them very small but delicious; small beans laced with garlic and ginger was the second course, a spicy meat followed that then cabbage with ginger, then the white suckling pig which was served with a wonderful sweet fruit.. I tried a little wine, half a glass, in response to a Gambai, it was not Grand Cru. But had we tempered the *Mao Tie*.

The meal went on, we had the odd thank you speeches, and suddenly something was said from the top table and all the Chinese virtually sprinted for the door. All of the foreigners were left staring at their retreating backs.

In all my nine years of working in China I could never quite understand why the banquets always finished with a mass exodus by the Chinese within seconds of finishing.

We went out of the building and the Chinese were all packing into lorries in the huge square – army lorries it appeared. They were again standing up all muffled in great coats. We started on the short walk to our hotel. We had an Italian contingent at the exhibition and we had met the main agent previously. He joined us, he had on a light macintosh, and a trilby hat. He was so cold he filled his mouth with cigarettes and lit them all desperately trying to keep warm. My brains were freezing – someone had told me they would!

I did get quite close to Bing during my stay and he was a very well educated man with a degree in English and was also studying law at the time. Following the reading of my book given by the vicar I did question him on religion in China. He told me that churches were not too plentiful in Beijing nor, he believed, in the country, nor were there many people that would discuss religion. As he understood it there were three types of Christians. The leaders of the Three Self Patriotic Movement (TSPM) who believed that it was necessary for a church in the communist society to accept fully the leadership of the government. They said they were 'called' to build up the body of Christ for the first time in history in a socialist society which was semi-colonial and semi-feudal. They saw themselves as the only true voice of the church in China.

Secondly there were those Christians who refused to join the TSPM, they affirmed their love of the country but did not think that the church should be a place for political discussion even though they recognised that there were many true Christians within the official church, these were in regular house groups.

Thirdly there were those not associated with any organised church groups but who met from time to time with friends in their homes – secretly because of previous trouble and some discrimination in their places of work. These were mainly in the big cities.

Phew...I loved the friendship store, it was only a short walk from my hotel, my case had plenty of space due to the mass of brochures I had brought with me and I was in the mood to fill that space with cashmere sweaters and silk ties which were plentiful and very cheap.

I was highly amused in the hotel. Dr Deaths secretary had arranged two coaches each day to take us to and return from the exhibition – most of the exhibitors staff stayed at the Jingoa. When we returned at the end of the day we would queue up for our room keys. The five girls would stand behind the desk waiting for us. Everyone would get into the 'Luby' line, just to get that wonderful smile and probably ask her out.

The main social club in Beijing was 'The Bell Club' where the Brits could congregate and get a drink or play a bit of snooker. The main attraction was the Shell Oil manager's three daughters, they never appeared whilst I was there but apparently when they did they were very popular.

BUT. Here I was sitting in a smoke filled room somewhere in Beijing listening to three conversations about exhibition badges, travel, Italians and interpreters. I had a very good camera in my shoulder bag and I was longing to go back up the dusty street to photograph women road sweepers, with plastic bags over their heads. I could entirely sympathise with them as the smothering dusty atmosphere in Beijing was getting into my breathing and I was longing to get back to Hong Kong for some fresh air.

The first exhibition was deemed a great success and one or two of our companies got to look at projects that were apparently to be developed. Offshore Tianjin was showing some oil so the main contractors vied for a chance to be involved. After much standing around and meeting dozens of Chinese, all of whom wanted to collect brochures and plastic bags, we eventually went back to Hong Kong for a bit of rest and then on to England firm in our belief that China was the 'big one'. On the way back, travelling first class thanks to B Cal, I sketched out the idea for my first conference and exhibition in Gaunzou.

CHAPTER 23

TOTAL ENERGY CONFERENCE AND
EXHIBITION IN CHINA. Apply here!!!

It was to cover all aspects of energy. The American conference company agreed to finance it and we collectively started promoting it first in Europe, then everywhere else. I thought it would be helpful to bring some energy related Chinese people over and give a series of workshops/conferences in the main cities in Europe. London, Paris, Rome, etc.

Dr Death at that time was almost a resident in China and we got him to invite engineers, purchasing, design, and project executives from the main Chinese energy related corporations and try to arrange their travel throughout Europe. Would the Chinese play ball? I had progress meetings with the Chinese officials at their home in the Red House in Blackheath. There were several Chinese there and they were most helpful and very determined to make the event a success.

We arranged for agents to work with us in the other countries of Europe and oversee similar conferences, all of us had alerted our governments and the UK Energy Industries Council were the official sponsors of the event ensuring UK companies were supported with some finance too.

With I.C.E. We had a team of sales people and very quickly got a good number of companies in Europe interested in exhibiting. I had also drawn up a list and contacted several worldwide potential speakers for the various sectors of energy to participate in the conference.

It quickly gathered momentum especially when we were able to inform potential exhibitors of the Chinese involvement. They promised all their energy related councils to work with us and we arranged for the mission, made up of designers, engineers, project people and government related departments to visit Europe armed with a view to discussing their requirements and the type of Chinese companies that would be ready to set up joint ventures and work with well-established European companies, that were already well ensconced in the energy sector.

In a limited way they would, but my first mistake was to put on the first conference at the London Hilton on Park Lane. We were reprimanded for choosing such a prestigious hotel by the leader of the delegation, I think the Chinese were overawed by the opulence. I also noticed that there were one or two that could speak very good English and seemed more interested in discovering what our companies did rather than talking about themselves. They still managed to spit at the slightest provocation.

We arranged workshops and discussions in the UK, Italy, France, Norway and Germany and had no real problem with getting many companies to register for the meetings. Meanwhile I confirmed a very powerful group of speakers from international companies to attend as our guests and in a short time we had a full complement of speakers that would descend on Guanzou/Canton for the exhibition.

I went in advance with two of the girls from the US company, we stayed at the Dong Fang Hotel which whilst being a solid four square building had a certain charm and an outside swimming pool that overlooked the exhibition centre. On each floor at the corners of the corridors they had a manned service station, with young Chinese ready to provide anything at all hours.

We prepared all aspects of the exhibition and conference, seeing that all the necessary communication and presentation equipment was in place. The Chinese were most helpful, nothing was too much trouble for them. I was given two runners that would be on hand for the whole programme, one was named Zing Zong Zang – English name John, and the other named Ling Ho. We called him Lennie and he was also contented. John was very bright, he already had a degree in English and was well on his way with another in law.

I was fascinated in the early mornings as I found it hard to sleep for very long and would get up early and wander into the big park just alongside the hotel. There were dozens of Chinese all stretching and bending, sometimes flailing their arms, but mainly it was very peaceful stretching and artistic movements, Tai Chi. Sometimes a mist would roll up from the lake in the middle of the park and ghost like figures would be there all seemingly completely concentrating on their exercise.

The White Swan Hotel next door to ours was also completed and we learned that it was being inaugurated whilst we were getting ready for the exhibition and a giant cover was being hung in front of the hotel dotted with fireworks. It was the most impressive opening ceremony with dozens of Chinese and a few foreign company representatives including some people I knew from BP who were going to have their offices in the hotel. For some twenty minutes the whole of the town was subjected to a variety of lights, bangs and swooping rockets. We were all then invited in to a major reception and there were the most stunning girls at each entrance smiling and inviting us in, apparently they had interviewed some two thousand girls and selected twenty of them to be receptionists for visitors, purely to just be there bestowing a smiling welcome.

The day of the exhibition dawned, our American directors had arrived, suddenly the hotels were full and most of the speakers were arriving. The conference element would take up three days – the exhibition was planned for five. John one of my young Chinese "runners", who spoke eloquent English became a firm friend. He was marvellous and a terrific help with all the problems associated with an exhibition and in addition would think out ploys to get the important Chinese to co-operate with any of our exhibitors. On two or three occasions after the ceremonies, dinners, banquets etc. I would invite him to join us at a very good bar we had found but he always declined saying he could not be seen fraternising with us outside of work.

When it came to saying good bye and thanking him and the other people who had helped, I praised him and said, "Everyone you are looking at the future leader of China."

"Ah" he said smiling delightedly, "I am from the same village a Chairman Mao."

Hong Kong was as usual ready to give us some R and R after the exhibitions and shopping was always top of the list. I had no problem in finding presents for my family. It was on the flight back that one of the girls said that our American backers were beginning to try to take over operations and arrange all exhibitions themselves. We then discovered they had head hunted and acquired the exhibition organiser of the Energy Industries Council and were intending to arrange their own programmes. The USA head man of the company was now permanently in London, conscripting experienced people and was aiming at getting a meeting with Margaret Thatcher to announce that his company was about to launch a series of high level exhibitions in China with the full support of our government. I should have realised that when I took him and introduced him to the Chinese centre in Blackheath, feeding him with breakfast first at my house when he told my wife he had been educated at Oxford and Cambridge that here was a man who didn't particularly care about impressions.

Carolyn and I decided to cut our bonds with the company and went to Hong Kong where we had met with a man who had a printing company, was respected by the Chinese authorities and did much advertising and printing for many of the corporations in China. We had met him at the Total Energy conference where he had shown interest in working with us in exhibitions, not that he had much experience, but he had the most important credentials, speaking the language and had an accepted business there. He was obviously successful, as he had an elegant launch in Aberdeen Harbour. After our initial agreement to work together he took us in the launch to Lamarr Island where we had the most superb lunch at the Lamarr Hilton, a tin shack with white wines standing in a window in full sunlight, and their own swimming fish in a large netted area outside the restaurant.

With our new partner in Hong Kong we then launched several exhibitions mainly in Beijing, Shanghai, Guanzou and Tianjin. Carolyn and I would help promote them and we quickly got progress. Andrew, our Hong Kong partner would bring Chinese delegates to Europe where we would set up workshops for them to meet interested companies and help promote the exhibitions. It was a very successful formula and we got government backing whenever possible. Plus we had contacts with other European agencies to replicate these workshops and we would boast that we covered just about everything from nappies to tanks in our exhibitions.

ONSHORE CHINA

I had another idea for an onshore exhibition in China. They already had several small fields in production but like just about every other developed country they were interested in further development and responded. I saw the magazine *Offshore Engineer* and persuaded them to have an involvement with it, in return for some advertisement about it. I was asked if I would report on it for the magazine and would distribute my observations.

We promoted it in the UK and also involved our other agents in Italy, France Germany etc. Obviously onshore was not as attractive commercially as offshore but we had a good number of companies from around the world committed and I flew business class with BCal to Guangzou. On the way over I slept in a very uncomfortable position and ricked something in my back. I was in some pain on arrival at the Dong Fang Hotel and my first interview the next day was with the director of Onshore China Corporation. My interpreter, Yang Ho – call me Yang please – introduced himself to me. He said he would be working with me all week. He was well known in the town and would ensure that I was kept informed of everything that was relevant to the exhibition.

We met the Head of O.C.C. He spoke reasonable English, and when I explained that I had hurt my back and was having some difficulty in concentrating, would he mind if I used a tape recorder to ensure I had got all the relevant points of our discussion. He politely informed me that he would not speak into machines and if I wanted to keep the interview we would discuss openly.

I managed to carry on and he agreed to open the conference and exhibition two days later, I thanked him for his agreement and on the way back to the hotel Yang insisted I see his friend at the main hospital and have acupuncture to relieve my pain. I was in no hurry to have needles pushed into me but he argued that if I wanted to be fully fit and able to cope with standing for at least an hour for the speeches at the opening ceremony I must get myself better.

He picked me up the next morning and we went off early to the medical centre. I struggled out of the taxi and we went into the centre which was huge. We came to what I guessed was the porters lodge, but in it was a very handsome man dressed in dark blue, he was the spitting image of Gene Kelly but with Chinese eyes. He greeted me and Yang and said, I was in luck as the leading acupuncturist in the world, Professor Chung from Beijing, was giving a lecture and demonstration that afternoon to many medical people at the Centre and he would be pleased to help me.

We went through various doors and eventually after climbing some stairs we arrived at Gene Kelly's flat, he ushered me in and introduced me to his daughter, quite a large girl, heavily pregnant. She spoke a little English and asked me to sit and she would make tea whilst her father and Yang would fetch Professor Chung.

After some fifteen minutes I heard voices on the stairs and in walked Gene, Yang, and a very old Chinaman in a huge flapped hat, and carpet slippers, he was apparently grumbling about having a toothache, and he only had one tooth. He didn't speak a word of English Yang informed me. I finished my tea and the professor asked me to sit on a chair facing away from him, he pulled out my shirt and rolled it up to my neck. The daughter brought in a jug with several needles swaying in it. I asked what he intended to do and Yang said he was going to insert them up my spine. I said I was fearful of this and was there anywhere that he could use when I could see the needles. They had some discussion and then the professor asked me to hold out my right hand, he felt around all the fingers and joints and then nodded, the daughter started handing him needles and he inserted them between the bones on the back of my hand. I told Yang that they were very uncomfortable and hurting. He said, no they didn't hurt. I only nodded. The Professor started to roll them with the palm of his hand and it was hurting, he then, through Yang, asked the daughter to fetch something and a few moments later she came back with what looked like a very large tight roll of newspaper, she struck a match and set it alight, he then started holding it near my back and I could smell the hairs burning and I was sure some smoke wafted over my shoulders as he moved it up and down. She then gave him the jug and he moistened his hands with the liquid that was in it, some sort of oil and proceeded to massage my back. Then he rolled the needles again and I was getting used to the pain. Suddenly he stood up and talked to Yang who said the professor wanted to dance with me – would I copy his movements. So here I was with a load of needles sticking out of my hand and I was doing some sort of dance movement with the professor. He smiled at me with his lonely tooth and after a few minutes of trying to bend my body he indicated that I sit down. He gently took the needles out of my hand and then pressed each joint on my fingers and also in the places where the needles had been. He also, with a single figure, pressed where the pain was. Then with a sweep of his hand he removed his floppy hat gave me a huge one tooth smile and shook my hand. Turning to Yang he said it is now 10 am he (*me*) will be totally better at 12 o'clock.

Already I felt some relief and I asked Yang to enquire how much I owe, both Gene and the Professor shook their heads and insisted that I could not pay anything. I asked if the professor smokes as most of China's men seemed too, yes he does. I then told Yang that tomorrow I would get a box of cigarettes delivered to him.

With many handshakes and smiles we departed and I could already walk upright and I was feeling much more like my usual self. We went to the exhibition and it was virtually completely set up so we walked around the whole site and told the first timers to have many brochures on show because the Chinese love to collect plastic bags and brochures.

At about 11.30 I was totally better. I was so grateful to Yang for insisting on getting me to agree to having acupuncture. The rest of the day flew past and that night we were again having a 12 course banquet, and Yang was able to accompany me.

He said that I would have to talk to everyone about the oil industry, how it has developed in the UK and what output is there from onshore fields. The two girls who worked for us offered to help write some of the speech for me. I said I could pan it. But several *MaoTies* later I was sitting between them and when it was time for me to stand, my legs wouldn't function too well, so I got them, through whispered words to give me a heave, and I was up talking about Aberdeen and how its developed and perhaps China would very shortly also be developing an offshore industry, comparing the two. Yang was interpreting, then I briefly covered Lincolnshire which has some onshore production and ended up congratulating China on its forward looking plans for oil development. Some applause rolled out and suddenly all the Chinese bolted for the door. *Phew, did I frighten them?* I asked Yang. No sir with a little help from me you made a big impression.

The next day the usual long line of blue clad Chinese were in a straggling line along the front of the exhibition centre. Dr Death had rolled up, not that I had invited him and he talked to them all in their tongue. Then it was the turn of the O.C.C Director, who clearly was enjoying his role and he talked for some twenty minutes – I noticed from frequent glances at my wrist. Three other Chinamen carried on with the reception speeches and then Dr Death announced that the exhibition is open. The dozens of Chinese who have been politely listening to their leaders speeches raced for the entrance and I with our two girls took a leisurely walk to our stand and watched the flurry of activity.

It was four days of high activity, several meetings with Chinese officials and some of the exhibitors. I, with Yang, would begin with introductions then leave the exhibitors to be handled by Yang. They all were very impressed with Yang's knowledge and ability to help even with the most technical aspects of their discussions. I discovered near the end of the week that Yang was very high up in the party in the area and much respected by all. He was very calm and completely at ease with everyone.

In addition to several other exhibitions we had contracted to do our second Aircraft Exhibition in Beijing, in 1989, our first had been limited in numbers but very successful for the Chinese. This one would include flypasts, for aircraft from many countries, a bit like Farnborough which we had studied when Andrew came over to see for himself how it was conducted – we had our own stand there. We had already provisionally accepted some six hundred companies worldwide taking space as potential for the exhibition when the revolt in Tiananmen Square happened. The sight of tanks running down students caused chaos and most of the companies withdrew immediately. We realised it would be a disaster so it was cancelled. Andrew was particularly upset as he had invested much time and money with the Chinese authorities as well as promoting it with us worldwide.

We were also hit financially and it was then that I decided I did not want to work with the Chinese anymore and handed all responsibility to Carolyn for future work. She was content with that and decided she would carry on with exhibitions.

CHAPTER 24

I left EAL, our company, to Carolyn. I then set up a new company from my home to promote Golf. In 1984 I had been invited to the Aberdeen Offshore Exhibition and the day before it opened the O.C.G.A. Oil Capital Golf Association were having a hospitality day, to which I was invited with George Williams, He was the first Director General of UKOAA. The Association of the Oil Companies in UK. George and I had become friends as he had spoken at many of my conferences. He had been MD of Shell UK before U.K.O.A.A. and he was a golfer. I had a rough idea of how to play, Simon the leader of O.C.G.A. had hired some clubs, but for me, it was try to hit the ball as hard as you can, which didn't impress anyone. We had a marvellous day, were entertained royally and that night after a very wet dinner a few of us were left sitting on one of the exhibitors stand's savouring malt whisky when I suggested to George that we could copy the OCGA's idea of a golf society in London with all the operators contractors and service companies making up a mix. He would be honorary President but he would have to bring the oil companies to an introductory meeting to launch it. We could call it 'The London Oilmens Golf Association' L.O.G.A. He agreed.

I returned to London then went to the Hilton on Park Lane which I had used many times for conferences and invited their Sales Director to be the first honorary member of LOGA. In return the Hilton would be our clubhouse and I would hold our first meeting there to introduce the idea of LOGA. I publicised the evening meeting and George informed me he had told all his members that it was being introduced. Forty four people turned up and George and I suggested the idea of monthly meetings at some of the best golf clubs in the greater London area starting in 1985. There would be a joining fee plus subs each year and any companies could have up to four playing places at any event. Each golf day would be sponsored by a member company. They would provide the prizes and get the resulting publicity. The RAC would be our first venue followed by Foxhills, Wentworth, and Royal Mid Surrey. I had talked to each club and made provisional bookings. Thirty five companies joined that evening, we were all delighted.

It also meant I might get some exercise as I was flying to China several times a year. It wouldn't take up much time and my secretary could do all the letter writing to members with the days programmes.

LOGA is a very successful association and is still, in 2015, a very active organisation.

When I finished with China in 1989 I then launched the UK Oil Industry Golf Championship. This was open to any golfers in the entire oil industry. There is a group in Norfolk. The N.S.P.G.A., North Sea Petroleum Golf Association. O.C.G.A. in Aberdeen and L.O.G.A. in

London, We all agreed to promote the U.K.O.I.G.C. with qualifying rounds and eventually winning a place at the Belfry for the finals each year. The Championship would be sponsored each year by an oil company and BP were our first sponsors.

The Championship took off and we had two qualifiers in Aberdeen, over fifty players fought for the ten qualifying places each day, The same happened on Gorleston where NSPGA house their events. We had five qualifiers in London, some of them coupled to a LOGA day. Ninety two players descended on the famous Brabazon Course at the Belfry and the finals were held over two days.

Also in 1990 I launched, The Forecourt Golf Society, based on the same principle as L.O.G.A. but for the downstream side of the industry, again holding monthly meetings at impressive clubs but travelling much more throughout the country as many of the members were in the midlands and north.

During this time I started an annual golf event in France, the UK Oil Industry versus The French Industry and would get it sponsored by either a UK company or Total, These were over the second bank holiday in May and initially I held them in Le Touquet, until I met a Dave Hodgson who suggested I hold them in Deauville, and he took me there, introduced me to Foie Gras washed down with a sweet white wine and I couldn't resist. He arranged all my travel through his company and they were extremely joyful and entertaining events. When the French Oil industry was finely tuned and most of their companies under one name we stopped but meanwhile Dave had started charitable events in France with some of the London Football clubs so I was invited to these and Dave being a superb jazz musician would sometimes play through the night. These were feisty times and mingling with the great and good famous footballers very entertaining.

In 2011 I sold the brand name UKOIGC. Forecourt Golf has shrunk due to the recession but LOGA thrives and grows each year. My golf has improved and for a period over the last two years got down to an eight handicap. Last year at Sundridge Park I beat my age with a gross 79.

Is it time to put up my feet....No... This year sees an eighty three celebration...?

Our two daughters Frankie and Jess are now well established in their lives. They are both loving and caring and give us so much joy in their sense of fun. Frankie is a professional musician in World Music with her partner Pete. They have visited and played in Cuba, Brazil, Borneo and most of Europe. Every year they spend several summer weeks in France and they play as Mambo Jambo to delighted audiences.

Apart from a brief spell in a circus after university, Jess has spent much of her time involved with the caring professions and is currently signing for the deaf at a large school in Chesterfield. She also works in horticulture with people with learning difficulties. In 2009 she and her partner Fin produced Aubrey, our wonderful grandson who is the delight of our lives. Thereby hangs another book...

Some recollections during those years

During the late nineties we had a lonely lady blackbird, 'Blanche', living in our garden. She was very independent and would spend much of her time on the lawn doing somersaults, then as summer approached she built a nest in the mahonia bush and produced four eggs. It was attacked by a magpie when her fledglings were born, and she lost them all. She was most upset and just sat in the middle of the lawn looking sad. Three weeks later she built again in the Ceonothus bush only to have the same happen again. She sat on the lawn and just refused to look at any of us with her feathers all fluffed up. I went out to her, sat on one of our patio chairs and suggested she builds her next nest down the side of our house where I had built a sort of lean-too shed and shelf beneath the roof. I pointed this out to her and really tried to influence her. A couple of days later she was collecting sticks and leaves and building on top of the shelf and there was another shelf above the nest so it was well hidden. She had four fledglings and they all prospered, during the feeding time she became very brave and would come up to the back door if she saw us there, and I started feeding her from my hand. Then she took to coming in the house and looking around to see what food was available. We had named her Blanche and she was a delight, when she had seen off the fledglings, no sign of a male at all in the garden, she took up residence in the mahonia and she would always appear if I whistled. She would also fly very close to you if she was hungry, sometimes touching my head with her wings. I had many friends round to watch her in action. I would open the back door, whistle a particular set of notes and she would arrive from anywhere and plonk herself down on the lawn then run up to me by the door and feed from my hand. We all loved her and she became a part of the family.

One day Mary and I were sitting in the dining room when we hear a thump and looking up we saw a bundle of feathers sliding down the sloping windows and it eventually came to rest by the back door, on opening it I saw it was Blanche and she was shivering and bleeding from the mouth. We carefully put her into a little box with kitchen rolls to make it comfy but she very shortly died, we were both very upset and we buried her with many comforting words in the garden and I made a little cross where she was buried.

A little story that might set your heart alight. Summer 2014

I now get up in the morning with one aim, to talk to my new friends, who arrive at my door between 7.30 and 8am. He has just flown in from the pond on the heath and she has slipped out from her thick cover of our copse where she has her nest. I ask them if they are hungry and the usual answer is a loud quack from the very handsome fella, and a knowing smile from her, she is now known as Dolores and she is also beautiful. He is Donald. I go back into the kitchen and select some brown seeded bread, give it a soak, tear it into little pieces, squeeze out the moisture and return to the doorway where they are both standing side by side looking expectant. Tossing some down – she is ravenous and tucks in, slurping it up whilst he stands watching with his mouth open telling her not to get too close to me, but does she care? He then takes one or two pieces and she hoovers up the rest. Then they waddle off to the trees in front of our house and sit and belch a bit... probably fart too. No doubt they discuss the quality of the bread. She is hungry because for the last nine days she has been in the copse laying eggs and keeping them warm and I think her only venture out is early morning to have a good blow out which will set her up for the day.

A few crumbs are left and my friendly blackbird who has a nest over our archway manages to pick up the little bits before she goes back to her nest. Donald meanwhile, sinks his head into his body and catches up on sleep as no doubt he has been carousing with his mates in the pond all night.

All this is observed by my very belligerent Robin who has his wife in a nest in the ivy in front of our house. But the ducks are too big for him to frighten.

It's a wonderful way to start the day and I leap out of bed, excited to continue this relationship. My only worry is that we have some foxes around and they may cause grief but I have alerted the neighbours to be on watch and when Dolores parades her 12 or 13 babes, the usual number, we must escort them over the road to the pond on the heath.

A sort of postscript

It is now March 2015 and I am confined in my little study with my left leg heavily bandaged and up on a chair following an operation last week for a melanoma on my shin. This is the third op I have had in the last year or so, so that should be it, as the old-timers say everything goes in threes.

Donald and Dolores are here again this year making themselves known in the neighbourhood by arriving at our door and expecting to get their breakfast. The granddaughter of Blanche is often in the back garden gathering twigs and earth for her next nest. So nearly all is well with the world

Last weekend we, Mary and I, joined our great friends Andy and Reggie at Ffald-y-Brennan in Wales on a retreat. Andy has Parkinsons and it is his and our second visit. He has flashes of being clear and will raise his arms and run round the lawn to celebrate. He and the two residents of the retreat, Roger and Tish led me to ask to become a Christian and much support was given for what will I believe be a nourishing experience through my future. I was also very proud to be asked to be Andy's Best Man…Must check with the Guinness Book of Records to see if being 82 is a record age for best man. He and Reggie are being baptised in the sea on Easter Sunday and their wedding is in May in St Ives where they live.

Brian B

Made in the USA
Charleston, SC
08 August 2015